HOW TO
WRITE
ESSAYS

Visit our How To website at **www.howto.co.uk**

At **www.howto.co.uk** you can engage in conversation with some of our authors – all of whom have 'been there and done that' in their specialist fields. You can get access to special offers and additional content but, most importantly, you will be able to engage with, and become a part of, a wide and growing community of people just like yourself.

At **www.howto.co.uk** you'll be able to talk to, and share tips with, people who have similar interests and are facing similar challenges in their lives. People who, just like you, have the desire to change their lives for the better – be it through moving to a new country, starting a new business, growing their own vegetables, or writing a novel.

At **www.howto.co.uk** you'll find the support and encouragement you need to help make your aspirations a reality.

How To Books strives to present authentic, inspiring, practical information in their books. Now, when you buy a title from **How To Books**, you get even more than words on a page.

HOW TO
WRITE
ESSAYS

A step-by-step guide for all levels, with sample essays

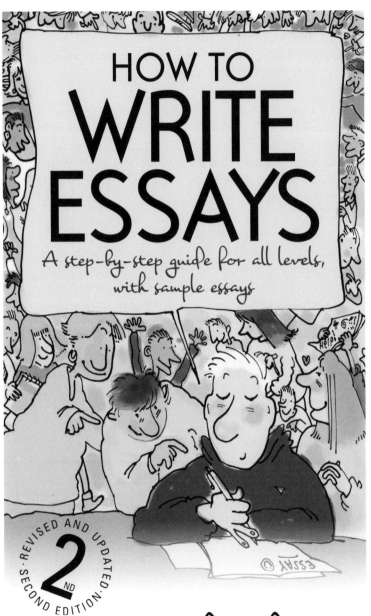

· REVISED AND UPDATED ·
2ND
· SECOND EDITION ·

Don Shiach

howto books

ACKNOWLEDGMENTS

The author and publishers are grateful to Nicholas Murray and the Rack Press, Kinnerton, Presteigne, Powys LD8 2PF for permission to reproduce *History* from Nicholas Murray's collection 'The Narrators'.

Published by How To Books Ltd,
Spring Hill House, Spring Hill Road,
Begbroke, Oxford OX5 1RX, United Kingdom
Tel: (01865) 375794 Fax: (01865) 379162
info@howtobooks.co.uk
www.howtobooks.co.uk

First edition 2007
Second edition 2009
Reprinted 2009

British Library Cataloguing in Publication Data
A catalogue record for this book is available from
the British Library.

ISBN: 978 1 84528 341 4

Produced for How To Books by Deer Park Productions, Tavistock
Typeset by *specialist* publishing services ltd, Montgomery
Cartoons by Phill Burrows
Cover design by Baseline Arts Ltd, Oxford
Printed and bound by Bell & Bain Ltd, Glasgow

CONTENTS

● ● ● ● ● ● ● ●

PREFACE

● ● ● ● ● ● ●

I strongly recommend readers to study and absorb the first five sections of the book before turning to the ten sample essays that have been provided. These sample essays are presented as models of good practice and each is followed by a detailed analysis or questions that are intended to focus your attention on key essay-writing skills that you should have learnt from the first five sections. You will benefit if you study these sample essays in tandem with the analysis that follows. Only with this kind of close attention to structure and detail can you hope you to improve your essay-writing skills.

Don Shiach

INTRODUCTION

● ● ● ● ● ● ● ● ● ● ●

The skill of writing essays is an essential tool if you are to achieve the kind of grade you want in the courses you are studying. This is true whether you are studying at GCSE, AS or A levels at school or college, or trying to gain a degree at university.

There is no single, foolproof method of successful essay-writing. However, the advice and the practical guidance you will receive in this book will provide you with all you need to know about how to improve your grade assessments by putting into practice some simple, but invaluable, principles of essay writing.

These approaches will work for you whether you are facing assessment in timed examinations and/or being judged by coursework assignments. In essence, the principles of essay-writing apply to both situations: when you are under the pressure of an examination room, or, at home or in college with more time to produce your assignment essay.

There is no doubt at all that the people who do best in assessments of all kinds are those who understand exactly what is required of them and who manage to deliver exactly that. In other words, it is not just what you know, but how you apply that knowledge when you are being assessed that finally counts.

In the case of examinations, you have to be effective at sitting examinations in order to maximise your grade potential. Like almost everything else, there is an art to taking exams. In other words, what you are being examined on when you sit an exam is your ability to sit examinations.

Equally, with coursework, you have to know how to present yourself in the most favourable light to the assessor. There has been a good deal of controversy about the role of coursework in examination assessment and how important a component for the basis of a grade award it should be. Problems of plagiarism from the internet and how to ascertain that students' coursework has indeed been produced by the students themselves without undue assistance have cast a cloud over the whole issue. However, it is highly likely that some element of coursework, however reduced, will remain an essential element of examination assessment. Thus, it will continue to be essential for examination candidates to produce coherent, well-written and structured essays for their coursework.

Essay-writing is, then, crucial in both instances: exams and continual assessment. In most subjects, a talent for essay-writing is essential to achieve high grades. Candidates who fall down in this aspect of their work will do harm to their own chances of achieving the higher grades. It is as important as that, not some optional extra you can add onto your knowledge of a subject. Essay-writing skills are an essential component of being a successful student at all levels.

My belief is that the basic essay-writing skills are not that difficult to acquire. The reason why so many students fail to acquire these skills is that not enough attention has been paid to teaching them. It is inevitable that schools, colleges and universities spend most of their time teaching the core subject-matter of a course, but hardly any time in advising students how to put their ideas down on paper in the form of an essay. Yet, these skills are neither obscure nor too complex for the average student to learn. This book will show you a method of essay-writing in several simple steps and will provide sample essays. Once you have learned this method, you should be in a much stronger position to face up to the demands of essay-writing in your various courses and across the subject range.

1
PLANNING YOUR ESSAY

Why should you make a plan for your essays? Why 'waste time' doing that when you are in a pressured examination situation or pushed to produce a coursework assignment?

Answer: Because it will pay off in the long run in terms of the relevance, organisation and clarity of your essay.

Think about occasions when in everyday conversation you are asked your opinion about something or about how to do something. Isn't your answer more likely to be well-received when you give the matter some thought before you jump in with both feet?

It is the same with essays, whether they are for coursework assignments or timed answers in classroom or examination situations. A little prior thought which is transformed into brief notes will pay dividends.

WHAT ARE YOU BEING ASKED TO DO?

Whatever the form of the assignment you are given, you have to focus on the specific task you are being asked to perform: **not** what you would like the task or subject to be, but the **actual** task the question is asking you to perform. Forget the fact that you know a great deal about particular aspects of a subject and <u>focus your energies on answering on the exact topic you have been asked about.</u> You don't make up the assignments you are set, your examiners do! So give them what they want, not the answer you would like to write, but <u>the answer you've been asked to write.</u>

That means <u>reading the words of the question or the assignment with great care.</u> Remember, <u>give the examiners what they want, a response to the task they have set.</u> Many a student has come a cropper by misreading the assignment or question and banging down almost all they know about a subject, regardless of whether it is relevant or not. Your essay may be absolutely brilliant in its own way, but if it's not an essay written in answer to the set task, then you can kiss a good grade goodbye.

Answer the specific question that is set, not some other question that you might like to be answering. Relevance is all!

EXAMPLES

- Consider this literature question.

  Why does Shakespeare's Hamlet delay carrying out his revenge for the murder of his father?

What are you being asked to do here?

To help you decide that, a useful approach is to underline three or four key words from the question. Why? Because that will focus your thinking on the approach you need to take and concentrate your mind on giving the examiners what they want.

<u>Why</u> does Shakespeare's <u>Hamlet</u> <u>delay</u> carrying out his <u>revenge</u> for the murder of his father?

Consider the words that have been underlined from the question. Underlining 'Why' reminds you are being asked for an explanation of Hamlet's motives.

Underlining 'Hamlet' reminds you it is *Hamlet's* motives for his behaviour that are relevant, not the motives of some other character.

Underlining 'delay' reminds you the question is about the reasons for his delay in carrying out the revenge.

Underlining 'revenge' focuses on the subject of the task that Hamlet has been given.

- Consider this history assignment.

What were the origins of the First World War?

What are you being asked to do here? What is your task? How can you give the examiners an answer in essay form that the examiners want? To help you decide, underline key words from the question.

What were the <u>origins</u> of the <u>First World War</u>?

By underlining 'origins' and 'First World War', you have focused your thinking on the events that led to the outbreak of the war, not some other aspect of the war or the course of the war itself. You may know an enormous amount about the First World War as a whole, but the only relevant information you need to answer this question are the reasons for the outbreak of the war. <u>Don't show off the breadth of your knowledge just for the sake of it. Pick and choose well. Sift through the knowledge you have and apply it in a relevant manner to the assignment.</u>

- Consider this Media Studies question.

Should the government intervene to prevent different media (newspapers, magazines, television and radio channels) from being owned and controlled by a few media moguls?

Consider what you are being asked to do here. What are the key areas you would need to focus on? Would these underlined words help you to focus on the task that has been set?

Should the <u>government intervene</u> to prevent <u>different media</u> (newspapers, magazines, television and radio channels) from being largely <u>owned and controlled</u> by a <u>few media moguls</u>?

More words have been underlined than in the two examples above because it is a longer and more complex question. The words 'government intervene' have been underlined to focus on who or what should be or should not be intervening. The words 'different media' emphasises that you are being asked to consider several forms of media. The words 'owned and controlled' reminds you the question is about who holds the power in the media, and 'few media moguls' tells you to deal with the question of media power residing in the hands of a few people.

By underlining these key words, you should have focused your thoughts on the specific question you have been asked to discuss.

Whether it be a coursework assignment or a question in a examination paper, the best way to focus your thinking at the start is by underlining the key words of the question or assignment.

Having read the question or assignment, always underline the key words that will focus your thoughts on answering the assigment appropriately and relevantly.

PRACTICE

1. In the following assignments or questions, underline the key words that would help you focus on what exactly you are being asked to do.

   a) Argue the case for or against the banning of smoking in all public places.

   b) Which is your favourite character from the set books you have read? Give your reasons for your choice and an analysis of how the character is represented by the author.

   c) How did the Vietnam War expose some of the rifts in American society of the 1960s and 70s?

   d) What does the term 'post-feminism' mean and do you agree or disagree that we are now living in a 'post-feminist era'?

2. Look at some examination papers in different subject areas and consider the questions. Underline the key words that would have helped you answer them.

MAKING A PLAN

Essays must have a planned structure. This is important for you, the writer of the essay. If you have a clear structure in your own mind, then it will be easier for you to organise your content and present it in a way that will represent your knowledge of the topic in the best possible light.

However, it is equally important for the reader of your essay. This will be the teacher or examiner(s) who will have to read your essay. It is essential that you make things as easy and understandable for them as possible. If you don't have the assessors on your side because you have made things difficult for them by your lack of essay organisation, focus, clarity and continuity, then it is highly likely they will down-grade your essays. Meet the assessors more than halfway. Make their job easy for them. Impress them with your essay structure and your methodical way of setting about the set assignments.

Any essay has to have an overall structure and make sense as a whole. However, for the purpose of instilling a structured approach to essay-writing, it is useful to think of an essay as consisting of three main sections:

1. the opening paragraph

2. the development or body of the essay

3. the conclusion.

As you would expect, the second section, the development or body of the essay, will be by far the longest of the three. However, the opening and conclusion of the essay are equally important if you are to impress your assessor. Without this basic shape to your essay, your reader will query whether you have supplied a coherent response to the set task.

From now on, approach your essays with this structure in mind: an essay must have a definite opening, a considered development and an emphatic conclusion. All three sections have to be integral to the whole and be linked, but for the purpose of inculcating good practice, think in terms of essays with three parts to them. The body of the essay will be much the longer section of the three, but this main section must be preceded by an opening section and succeeded by a closing section.

PLANNING AND WRITING COURSEWORK ASSIGNMENTS

Clearly, you have much more time to make a plan for an essay answer when you are writing it for a coursework assignment than when you are in an examination or timed essay situation. As you have time at your disposal, it would be silly not to use it to create a structure for your essay in the form of notes and a step-by-step sequence.

There are various ways of how to do this: the important thing is for you to find a way that suits you. Having read the wording of the assignment carefully and underlined the key words, as advised in Golden Rule 2, you can now move to the next stage: making brief notes that will help you write your essay using relevant facts and analysis in a coherent structured manner. Begin by jotting down brief phrases that come to mind that seem relevant to answering the assignment.

Once you have done that preliminary work and you have chosen what is relevant to the assignment, you should then make a plan of how best to employ the notes to create a structured essay. To do this you need to work out a paragraph structure for your essay:

1. introduction: opening paragraph(s)

2. first paragraph of the development or 'body' of the essay

3. a linked continuation of this development

4. further paragraphs as required

5. conclusion: a concluding paragraph.

The overall objective is to impress your reader (the person who is going to assess your work) that you have written a relevant, coherent and well-structured essay that answers the question that has been set.

In writing coursework assignment essays, it will pay to make a detailed plan before you start putting it down on paper.

EXAMINATIONS

In examination situations, where you are working against the clock and you have several questions to answer, you do not have the same time at your disposal to make such a detailed plan. However, despite the urgency that inevitably is part-and-parcel of any examination situation, it will be profitable to spend a few minutes making an essay plan, rather than plunging straight into writing your answers. Remember, in examinations, it is not how much you write, but the quality of what you write that will bring high grades. 'How much did you write on question 3?' is a very common enquiry of students to one another after the examination has ended. The implication of this question is that the longer your answer and the more pages of the answer book you have filled, the better you will have performed. That is decidedly not the case. An examination is not a competition among students to see who can slap down as many words as possible. There is absolutely no point in filling up booklet after booklet with answers that are not relevant or structured. As a former examiner, it was occasionally my sad duty to put a line through page after page of essay answers because they were totally irrelevant to the question.

Length of answer, then, is not the be-all and end-all. It is as well to remember that in any examination, you will normally only be able to use a fraction of what you know about any given subject. You have to reconcile yourself to that fact and decide what is most relevant to the assigned task from your body of knowledge about a given topic. Making brief notes before attempting an essay answer will help you to decide what is relevant from your overall well of knowledge and what is not.

When you have read the question and underlined the key words to focus your thoughts on what it is you are being asked to do, make brief notes in the form of words and phrases to help you focus further. These can be fairly random. Then take these notes and put them in the order you want to deal with them.

Now you have a structured approach to your examination essay. How long should you spend on this planning? My advice is not longer than five to seven minutes if the time allotted to writing the essay is an hour or less. You can get carried away making so many notes that you deprive yourself of vital time in writing the actual essay answer.

Allow time within an examination situation to make a brief structured plan for each of the essay answers you attempt.

PRACTICE

1. Look at some examination papers. Choose the questions you would have felt confident in answering and make a brief plan for your answers, bearing in mind the restricted time at your disposal.

2. Take some coursework assignments and make detailed plans of how you would write a relevant, coherent and well-structured response to the set task.

2
THE OPENING PARAGRAPH

● ● ● ● ● ● ● ● ● ● ● ● ● ● ● ● ● ● ●

What do you write in the first paragraph of your essay? We have all experienced that hollow feeling of looking at the blank page and wondering how on earth to start. Even professional writers such as journalists and novelists frequently blanche at the thought of filling in those blank pages with words. 'How do I begin to write this thing?' they think to themselves.

Think about times when you pick up a book in a bookshop or library and start reading the first page. The first impression you get from the opening paragraph might determine whether you go on reading it or not. All authors, however famous or experienced, give careful thought to the openings of their books. After all, they have to grab the attention of their potential readers. The first paragraph they have written might turn a browser in a bookshop into a buyer. If potential buyers like the first paragraph and it holds their attention, it is much more likely that they will make their way to the cash desk and buy the book.

You have the same need to grab the attention of your readers as these authors. The difference is the people who assess your work won't have a choice about whether or not to continue reading your essay. They are paid to do so. However, your first paragraph is bound to make an impression on them and will affect their view of the overall essay. Therefore, it is very important that their first impression of your essay is favourable. You don't want to have a reluctant assessor marking your work, someone who is really struggling to get through it. Therefore, it is worthwhile spending some time on improving the openings to your essays. Aim to make a good impression on your assessor with your opening paragraph.

'WAFFLE'

It is essential to avoid writing 'waffle' in your opening paragraph.

What is 'waffle'? It is when a student attempts to hide that they have nothing much to say about a subject by making generalised, empty statements that could apply to a whole range of topics, but which manage to say nothing relevant in answer to the question.

- Consider this opening to an essay:

  This is a very important issue and there are many different approaches that can be taken in regard to it. Many experts have considered this matter, but no one has come up with proven solutions. There are arguments for and against and many people feel very strongly about it.

What is wrong with this paragraph as an opening? Just about everything! It manages to say nothing, is far too general and non-specific, and the main purpose seems to be to fill up space and get that 'awkward' opening paragraph out of the way. In fact, it is not worth writing and is bound to make a bad impression. It is pure 'waffle'. The 'issue' is not even mentioned, neither are the 'different approaches' that can be taken, and none of the arguments for and against. It says nothing in 45 words! There is nothing specific in this opening paragraph, just generalised verbiage! It could be the 'waffly' opening to any essay on any topic.

- Here is another example of an opening paragraph that is pure waffle:

> *This question has perplexed historians down through the years. The historical circumstances are complex and the arguments and counter-arguments confusing. It is difficult to make a judgement about the main issues. All that can be done is to weigh up the historical evidence and try to come to a conclusion.*

This opening paragraph is not much better than the other example. It is all very generalised and non-specific. You would have no idea what the assignment was by reading this paragraph, other than it has to do with history. It is just filling space in an essay answer book! It says nothing! It is pure waffle and examiners will detect it immediately. So avoid waffle at all costs.

Avoid 'waffling' in your opening paragraph!

Thus, if you are to avoid waffle in your opening paragraph, what must you do instead? Well, you have to start dealing with the topic of the question or assignment from the very first sentence. Whether it is for a coursework assignment or in a timed examination, your essay has restrictions on length. Address the topic from the first sentence on, but don't try to pack everything into this first paragraph. You have the body of your essay in which to examine or discuss in detail, but you have to be 'on the ball' from the first sentence of your essay. Don't waste the time of your assessor by trying to ease your way into the essay. Say something specific in the very first sentence and

13

continue that for the rest of the paragraph.

Consider this question on 'Great Expectations' by Charles Dickens:

> *'In "Great Expectations", Pip has to regain his moral values after losing them along the way.' Discuss this analysis of the novel.*

The key words that you might underline in this question are 'Pip', 'regain his values' and 'losing them'. This will focus your thoughts on the need to deal with Pip's development as a character and involve you in considering what exactly is meant by his 'values', how he lost them and how he regained them.

How can you address the question right from the first sentence of your essay and grab the attention of your readers and convince them that you are answering the question as set? A useful starter is to use some of the key words from the question in your opening sentence:

Pip's values of kindness, industry, lack of pride and common humanity that he learnt from his childhood at the forge, through the influence of Joe and Biddy, are gradually lost by him when he comes into his 'great expectations', leaves for London and enters the society world he aspires to.

This first sentence mentions Pip, his values (four specific examples) and where and why he lost them, thus signalling to your reader that you are dealing with the topic as set by the assessor from the very outset of your essay. This opening sentence is not waffle, but is relevant and detailed. It doesn't just make some airy comments that could apply to any other novel. It is relevant to the book in question: 'Great Expectations'. It addresses the theme of the assignment. It is specific without going into too much detail at this early stage of your essay. However, it indicates to your reader some of the ground that you will deal with in more detail in the body of the essay.

Thus, to get off to a start that will reassure and impress the examiner, it is essential to get off to a positive opening and engage with the topic from the very first sentence.

THE LENGTH OF THE OPENING PARAGRAPH

As a general rule, you should aim to write an opening paragraph of four or five sentences. Your task in writing the opening paragraph of all your essays is to start responding immediately to the topic of the essay and to indicate in this opening paragraph what approach you are going to take in the remainder of the essay. You do not attempt to write an answer to the assignment in the opening paragraph. However, you do tell your reader/assessor what you are going to do and then in the body of the essay be as good as your word, before rounding your essay off with a conclusion.

Let us continue with the opening paragraph on 'Great Expectations':

> *The false values of Miss Havisham and Estella lead Pip into superficiality and snobbery, and a rejection of Joe and the honest, simple values the blacksmith stands for. It is his realisation that it is the convict he had rescued all those years ago on the marshes and not Miss Havisham who is his benefactor that brings him face to face with what kind of man he has become in London. His moral journey is complete when he faces up to his responsibility for Magwitch and regains his moral values.*

These are clear statements about how the character of Pip develops through the novel and the opening paragraph also indicates to the reader what areas you are going to have to cover in the body of the essay to justify in detail what you have stated. It is specific in mentioning the 'false values' of Miss Havisham and Estella and the counter-values of Joe. It also mentions specifically the convict, Magwitch, and uses the phrase 'his moral values' which echoes the wording of the question.

This opening paragraph clearly maps out how you are going to answer the question in the body of the essay. Your responsibility to your reader is to follow through on what you have promised to do: analyse in the development or body of the essay Pip's moral journey in detail with close references to the text of the novel.

USEFUL PHRASES

In your opening paragraphs, you can usefully emphasise the approach you are going to take by using phrases such as:

In this essay I intend to explore ...

This essay will discuss ...

This essay will focus on ...

In order to discuss ..., I will analyse ...

Here is an alternative opening to the 'Great Expectations' answer using the first example above:

In this essay, I intend to explore what values Pip learnt in his childhood from Joe Gargery and Biddy and how he lost contact with those values once his life was transformed and he left for London.

This opening sentence has the merit of telling your reader what territory you intend to cover in the body of the essay, addressing the question that has been set, and using some of the key words of the assignment itself. By the use of the opening 'In this essay, I intend to explore …', you get the essay off to a brisk, direct and specific start.

You do not need to use phrases like those listed above, but they are tried-and-trusted means of getting your essay off to a lively and focused start. You may have your own favourite ways of opening. The important point is that you start your essays positively with a sense of purpose and relevance that communicates itself to the reader.

Focus on the topic from the first sentence on, be specific in relating to the key areas of the topic and map out the ground you intend to cover in the body of your essay.

PRACTICE

1. Write the opening paragraphs of essays written in response to these assignment topics:

   a) *'The warming of the planet is the most serious issue that faces mankind today.' Discuss this statement.*

   b) *'Celebrity culture is a prominent and unwelcome feature of contemporary society.' Discuss.*

   c) *'Torture can never be condoned in any circumstances by a civilised country.' Discuss this statement making your own point of view clear.*

2. Look at past examination papers in the subjects you are studying. Choose some questions and write opening paragraphs in response to them.

MORE OPENING PARAGRAPHS

EXAMPLE 1

- Consider this assignment:

Should the voting age be lowered to sixteen? Write an essay that weighs up the arguments for and against this action.

The key words and phrases in the assignment question are: 'voting age', 'sixteen', 'weighs up', 'arguments for and against'. These should be underlined before making brief notes to focus your thoughts. Then you must write an opening paragraph that addresses the topic immediately, is specific and maps out for your reader the kind of approach you intend to take.

Your first task is to write an impressive opening sentence, which gets the essay off to a brisk start and grabs the reader's attention:

Debate about the age at which young people should be allowed to vote usually centres on the issue of whether or not they are mature enough to make a reasoned judgement about how to use their vote.

This opening sentence refers to the terms of the assignment (voting age, young people) and focuses on one of the issues that is usually raised when this topic is discussed. It also has the merit of directness and clarity. The point about maturity is flagged up for the reader and expectations that this issue will be addressed later in the essay have been raised.

Second sentence:

However, this raises the question of whether most

voters of whatever age make their voting choice after a process of mature judgement or whether they usually vote in the way they do out of habit or based on some prejudice of one kind or another.

This second sentence naturally follows on from the opening sentence and again indicates to the reader that this point about mature judgements will be addressed later in the essay.

Third sentence:

It is questionable whether so-called maturity is an issue at all when discussing when to allow citizens the right to vote.

This third sentence raises the issue of whether maturity is, in fact, an issue at all in this debate. Again, it seems a logical extension of what has been raised in the first two sentences.

Fourth sentence:

More central to the debate, perhaps, is a discussion of the innate rights of citizens in a democratic society, whatever their age may be.

This final sentence of the opening paragraph specifically raises the issue of the rights of citizenship, which clearly will have to be developed later in the body of the essay.

Thus, this opening paragraph consists of these sentences:

Debate about the age at which young people should be allowed to vote usually centres on the issue of whether or not they are mature enough to make a reasoned judgement about how to use their vote.

However, this raises the question of whether most voters of whatever age make their voting choice after a process of mature judgement or whether they usually vote in the way they do out of habit or based on some prejudice of one kind or another. It is questionable whether so-called maturity is an issue at all when discussing when to allow citizens the right to vote. More central to the debate, perhaps, is a discussion of the innate rights of citizens in a democratic society, whatever their age may be.

In your opinion, does the opening sentence of the paragraph meet the standards we have recommended? Does it address the question immediately, is it specific enough, does it map out the ground to be covered later in the essay and does it grab the attention of the reader/assessor?

Does the opening paragraph avoid 'waffle'? If so, how?

Do the remaining three sentences of the paragraph also perform the function of mapping out the territory that will be covered later in the essay? If so, how?

How impressive is this opening paragraph to the essay? Is there any way it could be improved on? How?

EXAMPLE 2

- Consider this assignment:

  'Many American and British movies are too violent. Censorship controls should be strengthened in an attempt to decrease the level of violence represented in contemporary films.' Discuss this question using specific examples from contemporary cinema films.

20

The key words and phrases that would need to be underlined are: 'American and British movies', 'too violent', 'censorship controls', 'strengthened', 'decrease violence', 'specific examples', 'contemporary'.

Here is a possible opening sentence to an essay in response to this assignment:

> *The issue of censorship has been debated throughout the existence of commercial cinema from its very beginnings at the start of the twentieth century to the present day.*

This opening sentence addresses the question of censorship and makes the point that the issue in relation to the cinema has been a subject of debate for as long as cinema has existed. The sentence addresses the question immediately and makes a specific point. It is a brisk opening and is likely to grab the attention of the readers and reassure them that the subject of the assignment is going to be addressed.

Second sentence:

> *Two major areas of debate have centred round the representation of sex and the portrayal of violence.*

This second sentence follows on naturally from the opening sentence and pinpoints the two major areas of debate as far as censorship in the cinema is concerned.

Third sentence:

> *However, whereas the debate about the representation of sexual scenes has largely decreased because of changes in public and official attitudes, the question of violence in the cinema is continuously raised.*

This third sentence makes a further point about how public attitudes to sex in the cinema have apparently changed but the issue of violence is still very much current. Readers could reasonably expect the writer to return to this point later in the essay.

Fourth sentence:

The films of Quentin Tarantino, for example, with their extremely violent content, or the violence shown in some contemporary horror movies, alarm many people, causing them to wonder what the long-term effects on cinemagoers, especially the young, are as a result of watching such graphic depictions.

This sentence gives some specific examples, as requested in the assignment question, of violent movies and it also raises the issue what the effect of screen violence is on spectators.

Fifth sentence:

There is a wide range of opinions about the need for censorship of violence in the cinema, ranging from those who argue for no controls at all to those who believe that the depiction of violence on film encourages violent propensities in society and who want the authorities to impose censorship.

This final sentence of the paragraph mentions the differing views on censorship and describes the parameters of those views. It is again an issue that clearly will have to be dealt with in greater detail later in the essay. It also rounds off this opening paragraph neatly and relevantly.

Thus, this opening paragraph consists of this:

The issue of censorship has been debated throughout

the existence of commercial cinema from its very beginnings at the start of the twentieth century to the present day. Two major areas of debate centre round the representation of sex and the portrayal of violence. However, whereas the debate about the representation of sexual scenes has largely decreased because of changes in public and official attitudes, the question of violence in the cinema is continuously raised. The films of Quentin Tarantino, for example, with their extremely violent content, or the violence shown in some contemporary horror movies, alarm many people, causing them to wonder what the long-term effects on cinemagoers, especially the young, are as a result of watching such graphic depictions. There is a wide range of opinions about the need for censorship of violence in the cinema, ranging from those who argue for no controls at all to those who believe that the depiction of violence on film encourages violent propensities in society and who want the authorities to impose censorship.

How effective is the opening sentence of this paragraph in relation to the specific assignment that has been set?

Is the topic of the question addressed sufficiently in the paragraph as a whole with specific points made?

Is there a danger that the paragraph goes into too much detail at this stage in the essay or is the amount of detail just about right?

Is there a continuity to the paragraph with each sentence following from the previous one?

Does the paragraph as a whole map out the territory that the rest of the essay is going to cover?

Example 3

- Here is another assignment to consider:

'When football hooligans from any country disrupt an international tournament, the punishment should be the banning of that country's team from the next tournament.' Discuss this issue.

The prevalence of football hooliganism is unfortunately a very topical issue. However much the authorities attempt to stamp it out by means of preventing known hooligans from travelling abroad and by co-operation among police and security forces, the problem does not seem to diminish. Each time the World Cup or the European tournament comes round, there are assurances that everything has been done to prevent trouble and yet those hopes are continually dashed. It is overdue that drastic action should be taken to ban any country participating in the next tournament if the supporters of that country cause serious problems involving violence and racist abuse. This is the only way that the problem can be solved on a permanent basis.

How does the opening sentence of the paragraph address the topic immediately?

How does the second sentence develop the point and say something specific?

What does the third sentence of the paragraph add that is relevant and detailed?

What function do the last two sentences perform in the paragraph?

Does the paragraph as a whole work as an opening paragraph? Does it map out the ground that will be covered later in the essay?

PRACTICE

Re-examine some recent essays you have written. Consider the opening paragraphs. How could they be improved in the light of what you have learnt from this section?

Practise writing opening paragraphs in response to any of the following assignments:

> *Should the speed limit on Britain's motorways be raised or lowered?*

> *'The use of animals in medical research should be totally banned.' Argue the case for or against this statement.*

> *'There is such a thing as the "the glass ceiling" for women in employment situations. Legislation should be introduced to make sure women are granted more access to the top jobs.' Discuss.*

3
THE BODY OF THE ESSAY

● ● ● ● ● ● ● ● ● ● ● ● ● ● ● ● ● ● ● ●

Imagine you have started your essay with a relevant, concise opening paragraph in which you have indicated to your reader/assessor what approach you are going to take in answering the question that has been set. You have raised, therefore, certain expectations in your reader. You have, in essence, mapped out the territory you are going to cover in the body of your essay. That's fine as far as it goes. Now you have to fulfil the promise you have made to the reader. You have to come through with the goods in the body of the essay. This is the section of the essay where you will earn the bulk of your marks. It is all very well creating an effective opening paragraph and a convincing concluding paragraph, but these will count for little if the development section of your essay is unsatisfactory.

PARAGRAPHS

An appropriate use of paragraphs is an essential part of writing coherent and well-structured essays. Paragraphs are the means by which you order the material so that your reader can make sense of it and follow the flow of ideas as you present them.

Think about an average length essay that uses no paragraphing at all. An absence of paragraphs would make your reader's task much harder. Apart from anything else, pages of unbroken print without a break can be quite off-putting. Paragraphs help your readers absorb what you are trying to say.

You have to provide a direction for your readers to follow and help them digest what you have written. Paragraphs are an essential tool in that process. Paragraphs give you, the writer, an opportunity to move seamlessly from one point to another in a clear and ordered manner, so that your reader can follow what you are trying to say or express. Without paragraphs, your essays could appear jumbled and incoherent.

DEAL WITH ONE MAIN POINT PER PARAGRAPH

As a general rule, try to deal with one key point or aspect of the topic you are discussing in each paragraph of the body of the essay. If you try to pack too many key points into one paragraph, you will confuse your reader and be in danger of being superficial in your treatment of the question. Don't try to pack everything essential you have to say into one paragraph. You should aim to make one key point per paragraph and then elaborate on it.

Consider this paragraph about celebrity culture in contemporary society (see page 17):

Celebrity culture, then, is a well-established feature of our mass media. For example, programmes devoted to celebrities appear daily in the television schedules. Celebrities are dispatched to jungles or undergo various tests for our entertainment and we, the viewing audience, are expected to be fascinated by all of this simply because of the participation of these so-called celebrities. Television producers have learnt the lesson that attaching the word 'celebrities' to a programme can produce dividends in terms of higher viewing figures. Thus, we, the viewers, become complicit with this strategy because we supply the programme-makers with the audience they require to justify the making of the programme in the first place. Basically, if we did not watch the programmes, then they would soon cease to be made.

What is the key point of this paragraph? It is that celebrity culture permeates most of the mass media. That point is made in the first sentence of the paragraph:

Celebrity culture, then, is a well-established feature of our mass media.

We could call this the **key sentence** of the paragraph. Key sentences provide a 'key' to unlock for your reader what the paragraph is about. Usually, key sentences come at the beginning of the paragraph and our advice is to keep to that strategy. By putting the key sentence of the paragraph first, you are signalling to the readers what the paragraph is about. The more signals like this you give, the more coherent your essay becomes.

The point made in the key sentence has then to be developed and 'given flesh'. Consider this second sentence:

For example, programmes devoted to celebrities appear daily in the television schedules.

Having made the main point of the paragraph in the first sentence, you then have to illustrate what you mean by specific examples or illustrations. This is done in this second sentence. This is then developed further in the next two sentences:

Celebrities are dispatched to jungles or undergo various tests for our entertainment and we, the viewing audience are expected to be fascinated by

> *all of this simply because of the participation of these*
> *so-called celebrities. Television producers have*
> *learnt the lesson that attaching the word 'celebrities'*
> *to a programme can produce dividends in terms of*
> *higher viewing figures.*

These sentences give 'flesh' to the argument you are making by being detailed and specific. Having made a key point, you have then to justify it by example and illustration.

The last two sentences of the paragraph act as a kind of mini-summary of the paragraph:

> *Thus, we become complicit with this strategy because*
> *we supply the programme-makers with the audience*
> *they require to justify the making of the programme*
> *in the first place. Basically, if we did not watch the*
> *programmes, then they would soon cease to be made.*

The sentence beginning 'Thus' draws what we might call 'an intermediate conclusion' based on the evidence that has been supplied in the paragraph. This is signalled to the readers by the use of 'Thus'.

The purpose of the last sentence is to draw the paragraph to a neat conclusion and perhaps point the way to what will be dealt with in the next paragraph.

For example, you could build on this last sentence in the opening sentence of your next paragraph:

> *Audience figures are undoubtedly very important to*
> *everybody involved in the television world. Equally,*
> *in the print media, ...*

The first sentence of this new paragraph picks up on the point made in the last sentence of the previous paragraph. Thus, continuity or flow of ideas is provided for the reader. You have established a system of signals to the reader: this is how my argument is being developed, you are saying, follow the directions.

MORE EXAMPLES OF PARAGRAPHS

EXAMPLE 1

Here is an extract from an essay discussing whether or not funds raised by events such as 'Band Aid' do any lasting good to the recipients.

> *It could be argued, however, that nothing really has changed since the first of these events took place. There still seems to be widespread famine, droughts, deaths from disease and civil war in the countries that have received the money raised. Nothing has been fundamentally altered by the giving of the charitable aid. The funds alleviate, but do not cure, the underlying ills. Far from transforming the lives of the poverty-stricken, hungry people, the money seems to be swallowed up and the need remains constant. Many professionals working in the aid agencies query whether these well-publicised fund-raising concerts do any lasting good. They look to other solutions for the deep problems that face Africa in particular.*

The first sentence of the paragraph is the key sentence. It makes the point that is to be developed in the remainder of the paragraph.

Sentences two, three, four and five develop the point and give examples of what is meant (the mention of famine, droughts, etc.).

The last sentence of the paragraph introduces the idea that aid professionals are looking beyond the money raised by such charitable events. That could lead into the next paragraph where that point can be expanded on.

Thus, the structure of the paragraph is this: key sentence, then four sentences that discuss the point of the key sentence, followed by a closing sentence that summarises what has been said and looks forward to the next paragraph. The next paragraph could have this as its opening sentence:

> *These solutions include urgent action by governments of the so-called developed world.*

This sentence picks up on the point made in the closing sentence of the previous paragraph and the linking word is 'These'.

EXAMPLE 2

Below is a paragraph from an essay about whether young people should be responsible for their own future pensions rather than depending on the state to provide.

> *The welfare state was meant to provide for the needs of all citizens from the cradle to the grave. When it was established after the Second World War, that was the laudable aim. However, changing demographics and the increase in the proportion of citizens living well into their eighties have put an unforeseen strain on the public purse. Hence, politicians are now saying the country cannot afford to carry such a burden of pension pay-outs. People, and particularly young people in their twenties, are going to have to plan for their own retirement*

pension so that they can live a decent life without fear of poverty. They will no longer be able to look to the State to provide adequate provision for their old age. The State, it seems, is going to opt out well before they reach the grave.

The key sentence of the paragraph is the first sentence. It makes the point about the expectations raised by the welfare state.

That point is developed in sentences two, three, four, five and six by emphasising the difficulties caused by changing life spans, the problems that causes and the implications for young people. The last sentence acts as a kind of summary and echoes the first sentence of the paragraph.

EXAMPLE 3

Below is a paragraph from an essay which is discussing whether or not the BBC should no longer be funded by the money raised by television and radio licences.

Those who profit from working and owning shares in commercial television and radio argue that the BBC enjoys unfair advantages compared to its rivals. The BBC, they say, does not have to operate in the open market like commercial operators do. Unlike them, the BBC is insulated against failure. Whereas commercial television and radio must attract audiences so that they can charge appropriate rates to their advertisers, the BBC need not worry about ratings quite so much because its revenues are guaranteed because of the licence fees paid by the general public. The BBC, however, argues that it has a 'public good' mandate which demands that the organisation makes programmes that serves the public interest: educational programmes, documentaries, serious news bulletins and the televising of important public events.

Sentence one makes the key point of the paragraph that the BBC enjoys unfair advantages over its commercial rivals. This point is expanded on in sentences two and three. Sentence four puts the counter argument on behalf of the BBC and points the way to the next paragraph where this point about the BBC can be discussed further.

The individual paragraphs of your essays must have a coherent structure: a key sentence that makes the key point of the paragraph, followed by a development of that point using specific example and illustration. A closing sentence should round off the paragraph acting as a summary of the paragraph's content, perhaps drawing an intermediate conclusion and/or pointing the way to the next paragraph.

PRACTICE

1. You should have written an opening paragraph for one of the practice assignments on pages 17 and 25 . Now write the first paragraph of the body of the essay. Use a key sentence, then develop the point made in that sentence in the following three sentences and then write a final sentence to the paragraph that rounds the paragraph off.

2. Analyse some of the second or succeeding paragraphs you have written in recent essay assignments and rewrite some of them according to the structure we have outlined in this section. Having done so, make a judgement whether or not they have been improved.

CONTINUITY

You must make it as easy as possible for your reader/assessor to follow the development or 'flow' of your essay. He/she must be able see a clear pathway through what you have written. Your essay must have the appearance of a continuous, coherent and integrated whole with each section dovetailing in with the previous section.

To help the reader, it is advisable to use linking words or phrases to signal where you are going in the essay. These linking words and phrases will provide signposts for the benefit of your reader. These signposts will benefit you too in terms of the grade you are awarded. The linking words and phrases you use will reassure your reader that you have an overall plan to your essay and that the content of your essay is being developed in a logical, point-by-point manner. What examiners don't want to read are essays that have no overall shape, seem to jump from point to point and follow no logical pattern. Linking words and phrases will, at the very least, help to create the impression of order and organisation.

Here are some useful linking words and phrases that you could use at the beginning of new paragraphs:

Another essential feature of ...

While it can be argued that ..., *it is also true that* ...

However, many critics disagree with this ...

To counter this argument, ...

Nevertheless, the evidence is that ...

Secondly, ...

The bulk of the available evidence, then, points to the fact that ...

On the contrary, ...

Having analysed this aspect, I would now like to ...

Furthermore, ...

In order to emphasise this point, I would like to point to ...

Moreover, there are other convincing arguments to back up ...

Therefore, ...

Thus, ...

Finally, ...

The purpose of all these linking devices is to help your reader see their way through the essay and to convince them that you have control over the shape of what you are writing and that you are thinking in a coherent way.

Consider these linked paragraphs on the subject of climate change:

Although experts disagree on the causes of climate change, hardly anyone disputes the fact that the world's weather is changing. This alteration in weather patterns has serious implications for our use of the world's resources, the emission of chemicals and gases into the earth's atmosphere and the basic question of industrial growth. It is an issue that cannot be avoided not only by world leaders but also the billions of ordinary citizens around the globe.

However, short-term gains and the selfish interests of individual countries and multinationals continually get in the way of controlling harmful side-effects from the growth of industry. Emerging industrial nations argue that they should not be prevented from enjoying the fruits of industrial development that developed nations have enjoyed for many years. Powerful nations such as the United States protect what they consider to be their national interests. At times it appears that there is no consensus about how to move on because every country is arguing its own corner.

Nevertheless, some progress has been made over the years...

The use of the linking words 'However' at the beginning of the second paragraph and 'Nevertheless' at the start of the third paragraph provides essential signposts for the reader to follow the argument that is being made. A continuity or flow is established for the essay that reassures your reader that you know where you are going. The linking words help to establish a flow of ideas in the essay. Every essay you write should have this feeling of continuity.

Consider this further example of the use of linking words and phrases between paragraphs:

Is it more important for any government to encourage through grants the creation of an elite body of sportsmen and women who can compete at international level for the glittering prizes of sporting success, or to ensure that the mass of the population have wide access to sporting facilities to enhance their quality of life and keep their fitness levels up in order to avoid ill health as a result of inactivity? This is a question that is frequently asked and usually government spokespersons provide bland answers about creating a balance between the two.

It is not as simple as that, however, because very often the provision of top facilities for elite athletes seriously depletes the amount of cash available to fund sports facilities for the ordinary citizen. Politicians have an inbuilt desire to curry favour with the voters through the achievements of our top performers. They bask in reflected glory when we win gold medals, implying that it is their policies that have brought about such success. Too often, perhaps, the needs of the population are sacrificed in the quest for prestigious prizes on the world stage.

In order to emphasise this point, I would like to point to the debate that ensues when our athletes fail to bring home the expected number of medals from world competitions such as the Olympic and European Games. There is always fierce discussion about ...

Paragraph two builds on the points that have been made in the previous paragraph; the use of 'however' reminds the reader that this paragraph is building on what has come before and that there is a continuity to the argument. Note that the 'however' is the eighth word in the paragraph; linking words and phrases need not be used at the start of the first sentence of the new paragraph, but must be somewhere in that sentence. Note also that, because 'however' comes in the middle of the sentence, it has a comma before and after it.

Paragraph three develops the point made at the end of the second paragraph. To provide continuity and show that there is a flow of ideas, the linking phrase 'In order to emphasise this point' is used and that is underlined further by the use of 'I would like to point to …'.

A continuity has been provided and the reader should be able to follow the ideas you are expressing. It is logical, ordered and clear.

PRACTICE

Look over some past essays you have written. How could the continuity of these essays have been improved by the use of linking words and phrases?

Use linking words and phrases at the beginning of paragraphs to help your reader follow the development of your essay.

THE USE OF CLOSE REFERENCES

In writing essays on literature, it is essential you back up the assertions you make in analysing a literary text by using appropriate close references. 'Close references' can be the mentioning of key incidents in a novel or a play, things that key characters have done, said or thought, or the author's own comment on the narrative and characters. Close references are your way of supplying the 'evidence' for analytical statements you have made. They are not the same thing as 'telling the story in your own words' or paraphrasing the narrative. That you must avoid doing. Close references must be chosen carefully to illustrate any particular point you are making.

Consider this assignment on Jane Austen's novel 'Pride and Prejudice':

What justification has Elizabeth for considering Darcy to be proud and snobbish?

Here is a sample paragraph from an essay answer:

Elizabeth has considerable evidence on which to base her assumption that Darcy is a proud, haughty and supercilious individual. Firstly, there is the occasion of the ball when he spurns the opportunity to dance with her implying that she is not attractive or interesting enough to warrant his attentions. Then there is his general air of superiority and his obvious disdain for Mrs Bennett, whom Elizabeth herself realises is a silly woman, but she still resents Darcy's lack of charity towards her mother. Most importantly, perhaps, there is the evidence of his marriage proposal to her when he seems to imply he has had to overcome considerable misgivings before he could approach her, given her comparatively lowly social position and the vulgarity of her relatives. Darcy has, indeed, provided Elizabeth with plenty of ammunition with which to shoot him down as an unacceptable suitor for her hand in marriage.

The first sentence is the key sentence of the paragraph. It makes an assertion about Darcy that needs backing up. If the assertion is made without close references to the novel, then it remains a mere assertion. Having made the assertion about Darcy, that assertion must be backed up by evidence from the novel.

Thus, the next three sentences of the paragraph allude to three instances when Darcy has behaved in a haughty manner. These are examples of close references to particular incidents in the novel. Note that brief references are enough; you do not have to go into great detail by telling the story of these incidents in great detail. You are not retelling the story for your reader, but using references to narrative incidents to illustrate a point you have made.

Therefore, the key point of the paragraph has been 'fleshed out' by evidence in the form of close references to the text.

Consider this politics assignment:

What factors led to the landslide victory for the British Labour Party in the 1945 election?

Here is a sample paragraph from an essay answer to that assignment:

The experience of the majority of the British people during the 1930s was undoubtedly a major factor in their decision to vote for the Labour Party. The Great Depression of the 1930s, after the Wall Street crash of 1929, had led to mass unemployment in Britain. With minimal social security available to the mass of the population, the working classes endured years of deprivation and struggle to meet the very basic needs of food, housing and health care. There was no safety net to fall back onto. Millions lived in wretched city slums and were seriously undernourished. The lack of nutritious food meant many children and old people, in particular, suffered from ill-health. Free medical care was very scarce and when the choice was between putting food on the table or paying the doctor's bills, millions had to choose the survival route and neglect basic health needs. And who was in charge during this decade of social deprivation? The

Conservatives, who were now asking the people who had endured under their government of the 1930s to give them once again their trust. The bitter experience of that decade, however, had not been forgotten and it would cost the Tory party dearly.

The first sentence of the paragraph makes an assertion about the impact of the 1930s on how people voted in the 1945 election. This assertion has to be backed up with concrete and detailed evidence.

Thus, the second sentence mentions mass unemployment. The third sentence adds further detail by alluding to the lack of social security and the key areas of food, housing and health care. The next four sentences back up this point.

Then, there is a use of a rhetorical question that is answered in the penultimate sentence of the paragraph. The final sentence of the paragraph draws a conclusion based on the evidence provided in the paragraph.

Therefore, the statement made in the key sentence is backed up with detailed and specific references that are appropriate and relevant. Whatever the subject area of your essay assignments, it is important to remember that assertions must be complemented by detail and specific references.

MORE ABOUT THE BODY OF THE ESSAY

It is in the body of the essay, then, the main section in which you try to fulfil the promise you made to your reader in the opening paragraph, that you will achieve the grade assessment you would like. An effective opening paragraph is essential and, as we will see in the next section, so is a closing paragraph, but if an essay lacks a coherent and detailed development, then it is like a sandwich without the filling. The body of the essay is where you will earn most of your marks. To earn those marks you must:

1. write in structured paragraphs, consisting of a key sentence that expresses the main point of the paragraph, followed by several sentences that develop this key point, using concrete relevant examples and references;

2. provide a continuity from paragraph to paragraph by using linking words and phrases;

3. leave the reader with the impression that you have organised the content in a logical, accessible and detailed manner.

PRACTICE

1. *'The internet is a very mixed blessing. It brings as many problems as it does blessings.' Write an essay making clear your opinions about the advantages and disadvantages of the internet.*

   Write a detailed outline for an essay in response to the above assignment. Pay special attention to the paragraphs that will comprise the body of the essay and suggest linking words and phrases that would be appropriate to provide continuity in your essay.

2. Re-examine some of your recent essays. How could they have been improved by structuring the paragraphs of the body of the essay according to the advice given in this section?

4
THE CLOSING PARAGRAPH

● ● ● ● ● ● ● ● ● ● ● ● ● ● ● ● ● ● ●

The conclusion of your essay, in the form of a closing paragraph, is just as important as your opening, the first paragraph. The opening paragraph makes a first impression on your assessor. Your final paragraph will be the last impression you make before the assessor grades your essay. It is clear that you must leave your assessor with a favourable impression. Before grading, the assessor will take stock of your essay as a whole, but the paragraph that ends your essay will definitely be an important factor in how it is assessed.

The function of the closing paragraph is to round off the essay appropriately. The assignment may have asked you to make some kind of judgement and this is where you have to express that judgement and summarise the reasons for it. It is wise practice to refer back to the evidence or arguments you have been making in the body of the essay. Of course, you do not reiterate the same points, but you must find a way of summing up that brings the essay to an emphatic conclusion and creates the impression that the topic assignment has been relevantly and thoroughly dealt with.

Look at the following concluding paragraph about what must be done to stave off ecological disaster:

> *In conclusion, then, I would argue that, unless all the countries of the world, great and small,*

developed or developing, powerful and not-so-powerful, make some sacrifices for the sake of the future of the planet, the resources we have taken for granted up till now will run out. The most powerful nations of the world, the members of the G8, must lead the way, otherwise disaster on an unimaginable scale might ensue. The time for empty rhetoric is past, the time for action has arrived. Time has run out for the procrastinators and the selfish. It is the human race itself that faces extinction.

This paragraph uses a linking phrase 'in conclusion' to signpost the fact that the essay has reached its final paragraph. The use of 'then' is another signal to the reader that you are reaching a conclusion based on what you have written in the preceding paragraphs.

Other appropriate words or phrases that can be used to signal this include:

Finally, ...

As I have argued, ...

As I have shown, ...

Therefore, ...

The bulk of the evidence, then, points to ...

However, as I have shown, ...

Based on this evidence, ...

The concluding paragraph must inevitably include an element of summarising what you have written before. Try to avoid, however, slavishly repeating exactly the arguments or content you have used earlier. Find a fresh and concise way of re-emphasising the conclusion you have come to. Be specific and detailed, however. Just as you have to avoid waffle in your opening paragraph, so must you avoid it in this concluding paragraph. Read the concluding paragraph above again.

Does it manage to say something meaningful and specific? Does it draw a conclusion?

FINAL SENTENCE

A neat, rounding-off sentence that leaves your reader with something to think about is sound practice in essay-writing.

In the above paragraph, 'It is the human race itself that faces extinction' performs that function. It is relevant to the topic, adds a note of finality to the conclusion and underlines the seriousness of the situation.

Always try to end your essays with some significant sentence like this.

FURTHER EXAMPLES OF CLOSING PARAGRAPHS

EXAMPLE 1

Here is a closing paragraph from an essay that is discussing whether or not there has been a tendency to 'dumbing down' in the media and mass culture as a whole:

Thus, there does seem to be considerable evidence to support the proposition that a widespread 'dumbing down' process has been taking place in the mass media and entertainment. The television schedules, as has been shown, are awash with programmes that scarcely trouble the brain cells of the nation. Equally, the tabloid newspapers appeal more and more to the lowest common denominator, concentrating on sensationalism, celebrity culture and lurid gossip. Most Hollywood movies, which, after all, dominate the world film market, are 'no-brainers' and devoid of any artistic merit. This essay has demonstrated that this has not always been the case in these three spheres. How this downward trend towards mindlessness in mass culture can be reversed is difficult to say. However, unless something is done to raise cultural standards, it is certain that our society will be the poorer for it.

This closing paragraph uses several words and phrases that indicates its summarising and concluding function: 'Thus' at the start of the paragraph is a signpost to the reader that the essay is coming to a considered conclusion based on the points that have been raised in the body of the essay; 'as has been shown' refers back to a paragraph in the essay where television schedules have been discussed; 'Equally' emphasises a similar point that has been made about tabloid newspapers; 'This essay has demonstrated' recalls the evidence presented in the essay that matters used to be different.

In this paragraph, the last two sentences round off the essay neatly by considering how this trend can be reversed and making a judgement about how important it is to do so. These sentences leave the reader with something to think about and bring the essay to a meaningful conclusion.

EXAMPLE 2

Here is another closing paragraph in answer to a question about whether or not the play 'Look Back in Anger' by John Osborne revolutionised British drama in the 1950s:

> *In conclusion, I would state that 'revolutionised' is too strong a word to describe the impact that 'Look Back in Anger' had on British drama in the 1950s. However, it is fair to say that it was of great importance, although, from the perspective of the present day, it is perhaps difficult to estimate how radical the play seemed to theatregoers in the 1950s. To make that judgement, the state of British theatre prior to 'Look Back in Anger' has to be assessed. As has been demonstrated, British theatre of the period was dominated by classic revivals and plays with almost exclusively middle-class characters and themes intended for middle-class audiences. 'Look Back in Anger', at the very least, with its 'angry young man' anti-hero, brought a new voice and language to the British stage. From the perspective of the twenty-first century, the play now seems rather reactionary in its values and gender politics. The fact that this was largely overlooked at the time is a comment on how very conservative British theatre was fifty years ago. In that context, it is perhaps hardly surprising that 'Look Back in Anger' seemed so revolutionary.*

'In conclusion' informs your reader that you are bringing the essay to a considered ending and summarising your arguments. 'I would state that' leads into your judgement about the topic. 'However' qualifies that judgement and develops that point. 'As has been demonstrated' refers back to points you have made in the body of the essay. The last three sentences round off the essay by assessing the play's attitudes from a contemporary perspective, which leads to a final word about why the play may have seemed so revolutionary at the time of its first staging.

EXAMPLE 3

Here is a concluding paragraph to a politics essay that asks what factors brought about the downfall of Mrs Thatcher in 1990 when she resigned after a leadership election:

The bulk of the evidence, then, points to the fact that the Conservative Party in 1990 had lost confidence in the Prime Minister to deliver another election victory. Too many Tory MPs, especially perhaps those in marginal constituencies, had become convinced that Mrs Thatcher had sunk so low in public esteem that she had become a liability to the party. Many were also extremely critical about her stubbornness in insisting on the Poll Tax to replace local rates, a measure that had been deeply unpopular in the country as a whole and which had led to serious riots in the streets of London. In addition, divisions about Europe were tearing the party apart and Mrs Thatcher's continual antagonism to the European Union was seen as deeply divisive. Added to all these factors were the personal issues of ambitious and sacked ex-Ministers who led the revolt against the Prime Minister and triggered the leadership election. Thus, a whole raft of factors led to her downfall, allied to the fact that she simply had been in office for eleven years, which is the longest any Prime Minister had served in that role in the twentieth century.

'The bulk of the evidence, then, …' introduces this final paragraph and indicates to the reader that the writer is about to summarise the points made in the essay and come to a conclusion. The following sentences emphasise the points made in the body of the essay. 'Thus' leads into the closing sentence of the paragraph, which acts as a final summing-up sentence and as a neat way of rounding it off.

Your essay should have a concluding paragraph that brings the essay back to the set topic and draws a conclusion or summarises the evidence. Your assessor must be left with the impression of a considered conclusion.

PRACTICE

1. Look at some of your past essays and having read them through, consider how your concluding paragraph could have been improved. Write an alternative closing paragraph to the one you wrote originally.

2. Look at some exam questions from past papers. Prepare a brief plan for one or two of them, then concentrate on writing a closing paragraph to these based on your plan notes.

3. Read some feature articles from newspapers and analyse how the closing paragraphs of these articles are written. Do they function appropriately as conclusions to the articles?

5
SUMMARY OF
ESSAY STRUCTURE

• • • • • • • • • • • • •

Your essay needs a beginning, a middle and an end. In that order!

The opening, usually consisting of one paragraph for an average-length essay, should get to grips with the set topic immediately. Avoid just filling up space with empty waffle. Say something specific without going into much detail at this stage. Your intention at this stage should be to alert the reader to the approach you are going to take in the remainder (or the body) of the essay. Your ultimate objective in this opening paragraph is to reassure your reader that you are going to answer the topic that has been set, that your approach is going to be detailed and structured and to get the essay off to a relevant and brisk start.

The body of the essay is where you carry out what you have said you would do in the opening paragraph. You need to write connected paragraphs, each of which should deal with one key point. Express that key point in a key sentence, usually the first sentence of the paragraph. Use linking words and phrases to provide a sense of continuity and development in your essay. Impress your assessor with the coherence, organisation and continuity of your essay. The body of the essay is the section where the close detail of the essay is found.

The concluding paragraph should round off your essay, drawing a conclusion if you have been asked to do so, but certainly summarising the content of your essay and leaving your assessor with the impression that you have rounded it off succinctly and neatly.

6

SAMPLE ESSAY 1:
A DISCURSIVE ESSAY

● ● ● ● ● ● ● ● ● ● ● ● ● ● ●

Discursive essays, sometimes referred to as 'argumentative' essays, involve you in putting forward arguments for and against a particular point of view. The skills you are being assessed on include clarity and conciseness of expression, organisation of the facts/relevant points, the ability to balance arguments for and against, and overall structure.

Essays of this type can often be rambling and unfocused. To avoid those faults, it is necessary to keep a tight hold on the development of the argument you are making and to back up the points you are making with detailed examples. Allow for the counter-arguments to the thesis you are supporting and deal with them.

The essay below has been written in response to this topic:

> '*Watching professional sport has become far too important for many people, especially men, and this obsession usually is a sign that something is missing from their lives.*' *Discuss this statement, making your own point of view clear.*

Opening paragraph

There is no doubt that the sports industry in this

country has grown massively over the last twenty years. [1] This growth is linked with the development of cable and satellite television channels, many of which supply continual sports coverage to subscribers. These channels earn huge revenues not only from subscriptions but also from advertisers who rush to advertise their goods and services when important sports events occur. The governing bodies of the various major sports in Britain, such as football, cricket, rugby and tennis, have cooperated with the television companies in signing agreements to allow the televising of their 'products'. [2] Thus, the amazing hype that surrounds major, or even run-of-the-mill, sporting events stems from the pooled and vested interests of the owners of the media outlets and the groups who control the sports themselves. This continual high-intensity marketing of sport has led to a nation of obsessive watchers, most of whom are male. [3]

Paragraph 2

However, [1] it is not only the people who watch most of their sport on television that are the fanatics. [2] The real committed fans are those who follow their team week in, week out, as they play around the country. What, it could be asked, is wrong with that? Is this not a harmless pastime that causes no one any problems? Yes, it can be, but too often this obsession with 'your team' can take over from a proper concern with other important issues of employment, family, relationships and even money. We all probably know of some 'sports nut', to whom the success or failure of their chosen team or individual sporting god matters too much. [3] Often

*belonging to a supporters' club or unofficial
grouping takes priority over relationships that would
appear to be more important in an individual's life,
for example, a wife or children.* (4)

Paragraph 3

On the other hand, (1) *such an obsession with
watching sport may arise because of a lack of close
relationships in someone's life.* (2) *Individuals find a
sense of belonging in a shared interest and this
bonding can appear to fill a gap that wards off
loneliness and a sense of isolation. In a group who
come together to support a particular football team,
for example, the individual may feel he is
surrounded by friends and other people who
understand and share his fanaticism. How healthy
and meaningful this may be is open to question,
however. If it leaves the way open for other
friendships and relationships to blossom outside the
shared obsession, then surely that does no lasting
harm. If, however, the shared obsession starts to
dominate an individual's life, then it could have a
negative effect on that person's emotional and
maturing process.* (3) *In addition, this obsessive
identification with a team can lead to aggression
towards supporters of other teams and this sometimes
erupts into violent behaviour.* (4)

Paragraph 4

*The evidence seems to show that the media, with the
co-operation of the world of professional sport,
continually and deliberately feeds this* (1) *obsession.* (2)
Consider tabloid newspapers with their extensive

coverage of the major sports, especially football. At times, in these newspapers, world events are relegated to minor importance compared with how Chelsea or Manchester United are faring in their matches, or whether England's cricketers can beat Australia or not. At times, it appears that the most important news at any given time is what has been happening on the sports fields. How many men turn to the sports pages first when they open their newspaper? And although there are fanatical female sports fans as well, what we are talking about here is largely a male obsession. (3) Often women complain that their husbands or boy friends can only talk with enthusiasm about the football team they follow. (4)

Paragraph 5

It can be argued, then, (1) that young men are less 'socialised' than young women. (2) This means they find social occasions more difficult than young women and forming lasting relationships more problematical. Boys too often are taught not to show feelings or 'weakness' so that there is a danger that they become guarded and withdrawn. Expressing their emotions becomes difficult as they mature. Becoming a fan, then, can make up for that lack because in the male group it is acceptable to show intense emotions on behalf of your team whether it be joy, disappointment, anger or enthusiasm. You are allowed to cry tears when your team does well or is defeated, because it is safely within the context of being a fan. However, outside that context, too often such a show of emotion would be dismissed as 'cissy'. (3) Watching professional sport can be an outlet for male emotions that are frowned upon in other situations. (4)

Paragraph 6

Nevertheless, [1] *we do not have to look far for evidence that obsession with sport can hurt relationships, frequently cause financial problems as money that could be spent on more essential things is lavished on the expenses involved in following your team and is a major contributor to anti-social behaviour such as binge drinking and violence towards others who are seen as 'enemies'.* [2] *When interest in sport reaches this intensity, it is clear that something essential is missing from an individual's life. Watching sport can be exciting and a way of bringing people together. Too often it is all-consuming so that fans lurch from extremes of despair to joy, depending on their team's fortunes. It is a diversion from real life problems so that when you are following your team, you can put out of mind serious issues in your life that need to be dealt with.* [3] *Many marriages, for example, have foundered on the rocks of sporting obsession.* [4]

Closing paragraph

In conclusion, then, [1] *I would argue that there is a distinct danger of too many people becoming over-obsessed with watching professional sport.* [2] *Statistics show that the number of young people actually playing sport has diminished, as the nation becomes largely watchers rather than players. We do not want a situation where the country is divided into two main groupings: professional sportsmen and women on the one hand and the spectators on the other. It is primarily a male problem, but the number of women who are obsessive sports fans is growing. There is the issue of the nation's health as well, with an increasing number of young people reaching obese proportions because they do not take enough exercise and eat too much junk food. The government must take responsibility for providing more sports facilities and offering wider cultural opportunities for young people especially.* (3) *Measures like those might stem the remorseless tide towards our becoming a nation of sporting couch-potatoes.* (4)

ANALYSIS

Opening paragraph

(1) This opening sentence addresses the topic by noting the growth in what the writer calls 'the sports industry'. It supplies a context in which to discuss the topic as set.

(2) Sentences two, three and four develop that point and give specific examples of how that growth has been aided by television, the advertising industry and the governing bodies of sport themselves.

(3) The last sentence of the paragraph makes an assertion about obsessive watchers of sport and brings the essay back to the central point of the topic. It also serves as a summarising sentence for the paragraph.

The body of the essay
Paragraph 2

(1) 'However' is used as a linking word to connect this new paragraph with the opening paragraph. It provides a continuity between the paragraphs. Note the comma 'However,' after this linking word.

(2) The first sentence of this paragraph is the key sentence. It tells the reader what the paragraph is about: the obsessive fans who follow their teams.

(3) Sentences two, three, four, five and six develop this key point. Note the two rhetorical questions (sentences three and four). A rhetorical question is a device to ask questions that raise issues that you will address. Do not overdo their use, however.

(4) The last sentence of the paragraph mentions the impact of such obsessiveness on relationships and provides a summarising and thoughtful conclusion to the paragraph.

Paragraph 3

(1) The linking phrase is 'on the other hand' which provides the bridge between paragraph two and paragraph three.

(2) The rest of the first sentence makes the key point of the paragraph: that the lack of social relationships is often an explanation for why some people become sports fans.

(3) Sentences two, three, four, five, and six develop this key point.

(4) The last sentence of the paragraph builds on what has been stated previously by introducing the idea of aggressive behaviour towards other groups.

Paragraph 4

(1) The linking word that creates a continuity between this paragraph and the previous one is 'this' in 'this obsession' which comes at the end of the first sentence. You can often use the demonstrative pronouns

or adjectives 'this' and 'that' as a simple device to underline the continuity of your development and to refer back to a previous section of the essay.

(2) The first sentence of this paragraph is the key sentence. It is the role of the media that is to be discussed.

(3) Sentences two, three, four and five develop that point.

(4) The last sentence closes off the paragraph and raises a point that is likely to be dealt with in the next paragraph.

Paragraph 5

(1) The 'then' after 'It can be argued' acts as the linking word between this fifth paragraph and the fourth.

(2) The first sentence makes the key point about young men being less socialised than young women.

(3) Sentences two to seven develop that key point.

(4) The last sentence summarises what has been stated and rounds off the paragraph.

Paragraph 6

(1) 'Nevertheless' is the linking word that provides continuity between the paragraphs and emphasises the flow of ideas in the essay.

(2) The long, first sentence is the key sentence of the paragraph.

(3) Sentences two, three, four and five develop the key point.

(4) The closing sentence gives a specific example of what has been discussed.

Closing paragraph

(1) 'In conclusion, then' signals to the reader that the essay is being drawn to a conclusion and that you are about to summarise your arguments.

(2) The first sentence makes your judgement about the topic clear.

(3) Sentences two, three, four and five refer to evidence that backs up the judgement.

(4) The closing sentence provides a neat and relevant comment on the topic.

7
SAMPLE ESSAY 2: LITERATURE

There is a method of writing well-structured essays that holds good for most subjects whether it be English literature, history, media studies, social studies or various types of general essays (personal/creative, discursive/argumentative, descriptive). The structure this book has recommended in the previous sections is not the only approach you could take, but applying it to your own writing assignments will stand you in good stead.

However, each subject area has its own demands in terms of approach and specific subject terminology. In this section essay answers to literary questions are analysed.

ESSAYS ON LITERATURE IN EXAMINATIONS

To answer literature questions in examinations, you should follow the same structure as outlined previously. It is just as important to have a clear opening, a structured development and a considered conclusion. The main difference between literature essays and other types of essay answers is your need to make close references to the specific literary text(s) you are responding to in order to back up the analysis you are making in the essay. In addition to close references, there is also the matter of the use of quotations from the text.

WHAT ARE CLOSE REFERENCES TO THE TEXT?

Close references are similar to the kind of details you might use in a general topic essay: they back up the specific points you are attempting to make by referring closely to the text, whether it be a novel, a poem, a play or factual writing of some kind. Close references are your evidence for your analysis or argument, the detail you present to flesh out your analysis.

Consider once more the question on Hamlet that we looked at earlier in this book:

Why does Hamlet delay carrying out his revenge for the murder of his father?

Here is a paragraph from a possible answer:

Immediately after his first encounter with his father's ghost on the battlements of Elsinore Castle, Hamlet appears convinced that the ghost is 'honest':

*'Touching this vision here,
It is an honest ghost , that let me tell you.'*

Hamlet emphasises to Horatio and Marcellus that he believes what the ghost has told him and he seems intent on flying to his revenge. Yet by the time the Players arrive at the castle and he listens to one of them enact a speech from a play, he is already beginning to doubt his own will to act:

'What would he do

Had he the motive and cue for passion
That I have?'

He chastises himself that he has as yet done nothing
about carrying out his revenge, comparing his
motives for action (his father's murder) with the
pretend emotions of an actor impersonating
someone in a mere play. At the end of the soliloquy
'O what a rogue and peasant slave am I', Hamlet
questions the veracity of the ghost mentioning that
the 'spirit' might be the devil who has assumed the
appearance of his dead father to send him (Hamlet)
to his damnation. This directly contradicts his
earlier assertion that the ghost was 'honest'. Already,
this early in the play, it appears that Hamlet is
looking for excuses not to act.

This paragraph uses a mixture of close references to the play text and direct quotation to back up the point that is being made: that after his initial encounter with the ghost, Hamlet quickly has doubts and looks for reasons not to act.

The close references consist of the details about his reaction to his first encounter with the ghost, his response to his meeting with the Players and their performance of a speech full of strong emotion, and the 'O what a rogue and peasant slave am I' soliloquy. These close references are essential to provide evidence for the reasons for Hamlet's delay. You use close references almost like a lawyer arguing a case in a courtroom: you make the point but you do not leave it there, but back it up with concrete evidence, that is, 'evidence' from the set text.

USE OF QUOTATIONS

As well as close references, quotations from the play are used to back up the analysis you are making. It is usually essential that you do use quotations as part of your 'evidence'. If you are allowed to bring the text of the play or novel or poem into the examination room, then you can refer to the text and copy what you need. However, do not overdo this: it is far better to use a series of short quotations or even one or two word quotes than to put down whole chunks of text.

If you have to memorise quotations for the purpose of using them in examinations, again it is better to go for short sections of a line or two at most. Answering literature questions is not a test of memory and a wholesale use of quotations for the sake of it is not sound practice. Quotations must be relevant and concise.

In literary essays, you must use close references to the original text to back up your analysis. Quotations should also be used but relevantly and concisely.

Below is a sample essay answer to this question:

Why does Hamlet delay carrying out his revenge for his father's murder?

According to the conventions of Elizabethan revenge tragedy, of which genre 'Hamlet' is a prime example, the main protagonist is duty bound to carry out the task of revenge that is given him. Of course, if Hamlet sped to his revenge immediately, then the play would be over very quickly, but the fact is Hamlet delays carrying out his revenge not because of the practical difficulties in his way, but because of his own emotionally confused and irresolute nature. Shakespeare represents Hamlet as continuously finding excuses for non-action. This essay will explore his professed motives for the delayed revenge.

Immediately after his first encounter with his father's ghost on the battlements of Elsinore Castle, Hamlet appears convinced that the ghost is 'honest':

> 'Touching this vision here,
> It is an honest ghost, that let me tell you.'

Hamlet emphasises to Horatio and Marcellus that he believes what the ghost has told him and he seems intent on flying to his revenge. Yet by the time the Players arrive at the castle and he listens to one of them enact a speech from a play, he is already beginning to doubt his own will to act:

> 'What would he do
> Had he the motive and cue for passion
> That I have?'

He chastises himself that he has as yet done nothing about carrying out his revenge, comparing his motives for action (his father's murder) with the pretend emotions of an actor impersonating someone in a mere play. At the end of the soliloquy 'O what a rogue and peasant slave am I', Hamlet questions the veracity of the ghost mentioning that the 'spirit' might be the devil who has assumed the appearance of his dead father to send him (Hamlet) to his damnation. This directly contradicts his earlier assertion that the ghost was 'honest'. Already, this early in the play, it appears that Hamlet is looking for excuses not to act.

In addition, Hamlet has already warned Horatio

and Marcellus that he may at times put on an 'antic disposition', in other words, he will appear distracted and even crazy. Why Hamlet should decide at the early stage that he might need to don this disguise is witness to the fact he already is daunted by his task. This is further emphasised when he states at the end of Act One, Scene V:

> 'The time is out of joint: O cursed spite
> That ever I was born to set it right.'

Are these the words of a son determined to speed to revenge his father's murder? They are more the thoughts of a man who is already having doubts about his ability and determination to obey his dead father's ghost and kill his uncle.

We have, then, to examine Hamlet's state of mind and emotions that leads him to this impasse. When we first see Hamlet on stage, it is clear that he is in a state of deep melancholy and that he is resentful of his mother's remarriage to his uncle so soon after his father's death. Claudius and Gertrude both try to win him over and to persuade him to give up the deep mourning for his father that has made him so withdrawn and resentful. He rejects the oily, self-serving entreaties of his uncle and is angry with his mother, accusing her of lacking real feeling in comparison with his own grief. At the end of the scene, there is the first of Hamlet's soliloquies when he contemplates suicide. Everything about life seems 'weary, stale, flat and unprofitable' and the world itself is possessed by things that are 'rank and gross'. We soon learn that what has caused Hamlet's alienation is his mother's marriage to his uncle, which he considers to be an incestuous union.

Hamlet is full of physical disgust about his mother's betrayal of his dead father:

'O most wicked speed, to post
With such dexterity to incestuous sheets!'

Thus, Hamlet at the beginning of the play before the ghost gives him the task of revenge is already in an emotionally distraught state, obsessed with his mother's betrayal (as he sees it) and acting almost like a spurned lover towards her.

Further evidence of Hamlet's disturbed state of mind is presented when he delivers his 'To be or not to be' soliloquy. He seems obsessed with thoughts of self-destruction and refers to 'outrageous fortune' and 'a sea of troubles'. These are the words of a man who thinks himself cursed to have been burdened with the task of revenge. He sounds like a man faced with seemingly insurmountable problems. His upset with the treachery of his mother and women in general ('O frailty thy name is woman!') is expressed forcibly in the following scene with Ophelia when he tells her to go to a nunnery and denies that he ever loved her. His words in this scene are wild and cruel and indicate that he is near the end of his tether.

However, after the play scene, when Claudius's guilt is openly expressed, Hamlet can be in no doubt that what the ghost has told him is indeed true. Yet when he is summoned to his mother's closet and on the way sees Claudius praying, he again fails to carry out his revenge even though he has had the final proof of his uncle's guilt and Claudius is unprotected. Once more, however, Hamlet finds an excuse to delay his revenge, stating that as his uncle is praying; if he were to kill him at that point, his uncle's soul would go to heaven. No, Hamlet reasons, better to find an opportunity when Claudius is drunk, in a rage or in his 'incestuous' bed so that his soul will be consigned to hell. It is true that in Elizabethan times, it was believed that a person killed while at prayer and in a state of contrition for his sins would be forgiven and his soul assigned to heaven, but is this not, in reality, another episode where Hamlet shows his reluctance to carry out his revenge? He is a man full of guilt about his own feelings towards his mother, which renders him incapable of considered action. Hamlet acts on impulse, which we see in the very next scene of the play when he kills Polonius thinking he is Claudius, even though he has just left the king praying and has turned down the chance of killing him then.

It is, indeed, in this closet scene where Hamlet expresses yet again his deep disgust at his mother's remarriage:

> 'You are the queen, your husband's brother's wife
> And - would it were not so! - you are my mother.'

Shakespeare could provide no clearer explanation for his hero's delaying tactics than in this scene. Hamlet is consumed with distaste at the idea that his mother has betrayed his dead father by sharing an incestuous bed with his father's brother. His mother, for Hamlet, is 'Stew'd in corruption'. At this point in the action, the ghost of Hamlet's father makes his second appearance to his son 'to whet thy almost blunted purpose'. This reminds us, the audience, that Hamlet had indeed dithered over his revenge. Before he leaves his mother, hauling

Polonius's dead body with him, he makes her promise to stay away from his uncle's bed. Shakespeare has him reiterate his profound disgust at the thought of his mother's 'sin'. Hamlet is a hero caught up in a deep neurosis, which he cannot apparently free himself from and which prevents him from taking considered action to revenge his father.

Thus, when he does finally kill his uncle, it is not as a result of planning but as an impulsive reaction to the realisation that Claudius has tried to have him poisoned during the duel with Laertes. As the King dies, Hamlet calls him the 'incestuous, murderous damned Dane'. At last, Hamlet has revenged his father, but he has never been in control of events, but seems to react impulsively to them. This is because he has been too obsessed with his own neurotic feelings to be able to act rationally. As a result, he has managed to kill the father of the woman (Ophelia) he once loved, helped to send her into madness ending in her death and made her brother a sworn enemy. The only victor of the situation in Denmark appears to be Fortinbras who arrives at the castle in time to put things in order and take control. Hamlet, by comparison, achieves his revenge but at the cost of his life and his mother's as well. It is this central relationship between Hamlet and Gertrude that supplies the crucial reasons for the delay in Hamlet's revenge with the tragic consequences that ensue.

ASSESSING THE ESSAY

Put yourself in the position of the assessor who has to grade this essay. Ask yourself these questions:

- Does the opening paragraph address the topic of the question and say something specific about it, indicating the kind of ground that will be covered in the remainder of the essay?

- Does it avoid empty waffle?

Consider each of the next six paragraphs.

- Do they each have a key sentence?

- Do they all deal mainly with one key point?

- Is this key point developed and backed up by close references to the text?

- Are relevant quotations used?

- Does the final sentence of each paragraph act as a kind of summarising sentence for the paragraph or point towards the next paragraph?

- Are these six paragraphs linked together by a linking word or phrase?

- Is there a sense of continuity or flow to these six paragraphs, the body of the essay?

- Does the essay indicate in the final paragraph that some kind of conclusion is being reached?

- Does the final paragraph act as kind of summary of the case the writer has been making?

- Does the final paragraph round off the essay appropriately, bringing the essay squarely back to the overall topic of the question?

8
SAMPLE ESSAY 3: WRITING ABOUT POETRY

When you write about poetry, you have to be aware that it is not the same as when you are writing about prose or drama. The specific characteristics of poetry such as concentration or weight of language, the form, rhythms and cadences, the figurative language and imagery, must be acknowledged and dealt with. Of course, prose at times uses figurative language and imagery and often has its own rhythms as well, so prose and poetry often share literary characteristics. It is possible to talk about 'poetic prose' and 'prosaic poetry' when one or the other is permeated with features commonly associated with the other mode. Generally, however, in poetry it is the importance that the language – or diction, as it is called in poetry – is given, the concentration of meaning that poets give their words, that creates the resonance of meaning that creates the effect the poet is seeking.

Indeed, whatever subject area you are writing about in essays, it is important that you use with confidence the specific vocabulary and terminology associated with the particular subject. For example, history and geography as areas of study each have their own terminology, their own specific modes of discussion and vocabulary. That is not to say that you should lapse into subject 'jargon' for the sake of it, but you should display to your assessors that you are aware of the kind of terms that are generally employed in writing about particular subjects.

Read the poem below by Robert Browning and then consider the sample essay that follows in response to the following question:

What, in your judgement, makes 'Meeting at Night' an effective poem?

Meeting at Night

The grey sea and the long black land;
And the yellow half-moon large and low;
And the startled little waves that leap
In fiery ringlets from their sleep,
As I gain the cove with pushing prow,
And quench its speed in the slushy sand.

Then a mile of warm-scented beach;
Three fields to cross till a farm appears;
A tap at the pane, the quick sharp scratch
And blue spurt of a lighted match,
And a voice less loud, thro' its joys and fears,
Than the two hearts beating each to each!

Robert Browning

Opening paragraph

In 'Meeting at Night', the poem is attempting to communicate the excitement of a lover as he hastens towards a love tryst with his beloved. Browning effectively uses the cadences and rhythms of the verse, striking imagery and the form of the short poem to express the protagonist's mounting excitement as he nears the meeting place and his lover. The lovers' embrace at the end of the poem has been prepared for by the intensity of feelings that have been already expressed.

Paragraph 2

Browning sets the scene in the first two lines of the poem. The monosyllables 'grey sea' and 'long black land' establishes a bleak empty landscape as background to the drama. He uses simple diction with long vowels to start the poem with a slow rhythm. This contrasts with the quickening rhythms and rising cadences that follow. The alliteration of 'long black land' and 'large and low' adds to the resonance of the verse. The rhyming pattern of the verse, which will be replicated in the second stanza, of a b c c b a helps to create the cohesion of this half of the poem.

Paragraph 3

By the third line of the verse, then, the cadence is rising and this is reflected in his use of metaphor: the waves are 'startled' and they 'leap in fiery ringlets'. The sea in the agitation caused by the 'pushing prow' reflects the excitement of the lover as he races to the meeting place. Even the use of 'quench' to describe the boat's landing on the 'slushy sand' only manages to reinforce the feverish haste of the lover. The alliteration of 'pushing prow' and 'speed in the slushy sand' helps to emphasise the tone of wild excitement.

Paragraph 4

The second stanza starts similarly to the first with a slowing of the rhythm and falling cadences: 'a mile of warm sea-scented beach' and 'Three fields to cross'. Then the short, almost staccato rhythms and the rising cadence of the lines that follow anticipate the climax of the poem: ' A tap at the pane' and 'the quick sharp scratch'. The images of the 'blue spurt' and 'lighted match' suggest the explosive emotions of the lovers. Browning effectively communicates the intensity of feeling by describing the voice of one of the lovers as being 'less loud' than the sound of their hearts beating as they embrace. 'Each to each!' underlines with the additional emphasis of the climactic exclamation mark the need of the lovers to be together again. As in the first stanza, the first two lines of the poem are end-stop lines, then the next two lines are examples of enjambement where the meaning flows without pause from one line to the next. The rising cadence of 'And' as the first word of both lines four and five helps to keep the flow of the verse going, underlining the intensity of the feelings.

Closing paragraph

Thus, Browning has effectively used the characteristics usually associated specifically with poetry - rhythm and cadence, concentration of diction, imagery and rhyme - to create a valid form for what he was trying to express: the intense excitement involved in two lovers meeting after a parting. None of the diction that Browning uses is that unusual, indeed, it is mostly simple, almost mundane, but it is in the combinations of words used, creating the rise and fall of the cadence of the verse, and with a subtle use of rhyming pattern , that he manages to create a short poem of two six-line stanzas that is an outstanding example of how poetic form and theme can merge successfully to communicate deep feeling.

ANALYSIS

The opening paragraph

The first sentence addresses the topic immediately and explains what the poem is about.

Sentence two mentions the specific poetic characteristics employed by the poet to make the poem effective.

Sentence three makes the point that the climax of the poem has been led up to in the preceding lines.

Paragraph 2

Having discussed the poem as a whole in the first paragraph, the essay now deals with the first verse.

Sentences two to six provide detailed analysis of the verse, using quotes and commenting appropriately. They also use subject-specific terms such as 'cadence', 'metaphor', 'rhyming pattern' and 'alliteration'.

Paragraph 3

The use of linking word 'then' links the previous paragraph to this one.

Sentence one is the key sentence focusing on the cadence of the verse.

Sentences two, three and four analyse the cadence in detail with quotes from the poem.

Paragraph 4

The linking word is 'similarly' which makes a connection for the reader with what is to be discussed now and what previous paragraphs have analysed.

Sentences two to six give a very detailed analysis with the use of appropriate quotes (note that these have inverted commas or quotation marks round them).

Closing paragraph

'Thus' is used to signal that you are about to sum up your analysis based on your detailed examination of the poem.

Sentence 2 gives a final judgement of how effective the poem is, but is specific in mentioning the features that make it an effective poem.

Specific terms

These are the subject-specific terms used in this essay answer on poetry:

- alliteration
- diction
- end-stop lines
- enjambement
- imagery
- metaphor
- rhyming patterns
- rhythm.

9
SAMPLE ESSAY 4: ANOTHER ESSAY ON A POEM

Assignment: Write a critical appreciation of the poem 'History' by Nicholas Murray, including a discussion of the poem's themes and the poet's treatment of them.

History

The tall girl from Kildare,
I imagine you among horses and wide fields,
Having taken the fence you faltered at,
Marrying your man with the stubbled chin
And the slow, gentle smile.
On our bar stools, just the two of us,
Like an emblem of innocence and experience,
We rehearsed your story: dismantled dreams
When his car left the country road
And your heart, untenanted, searching,
Came to ask itself if happiness was the four walls
Of a good man's house who would not survive you.

On a lift into town, he stopped at a barley field,
Waded out like a fisherman in shallow seas,
To stare at the blank horizon, as if a message
Were posted for his attention,
And came back to the Land Rover, saying nothing.

Our game of tennis at dusk, the lost ball we foraged for
In the long grass where our hands brushed lightly
And you turned away, saying nothing.
Do you rule now a flagged kitchen
In a big house among fields,
Or do you trim the plant of a single life
With expert fingers, sheathed in a green glove?

Nicholas Murray

Opening paragraph

'History' has an almost elegiac tone as the poet remembers 'the tall girl from Kildare' and tells the story obliquely of the loss of her young fiancé in a car accident and the dilemma she now faces of whether to put his memory behind her and marry another, older man who is offering himself; the alternative would be to live alone, tending her garden with no companion for life. There are various time-shifts in the poem: the time before the poet meets her, the time when they were close and the present when he wonders about what she is doing now. There is a sense of a lost love, a regret and a sadness which are expressed by the poet in language that is concentrated and resonant.

Paragraph 2

The first line of the poem immediately establishes who the poem is about. We are presented with an image of the 'girl' through the poet's imagination: she is 'among horses and wide fields' and is keen on horse-riding. The man she will possibly marry is evocatively described as having a 'stubbled chin' and a 'slow gentle smile'. Then there is a shift to a time after her fiancé has died. The poet sits with her in a bar discussing her 'story'. Her dreams of happiness with her potential husband have been destroyed and she is questioning whether she can really envisage finding happiness again with the decent but much older local farmer who wants to marry her.

Paragraph 3

The second verse of the poem records a moment when the poet, travelling with the potential new husband, stops at a field of barley into which the farmer walks to stare at the horizon. His silent, uncommunicative gaze, suggests a man of few words, a simple countryman who may not be sure that he is doing the right thing in marrying the girl. He knows that the poet knows her. Is he groping for some indication from the poet about what he should do? Probably not! The third verse brings the poem back to the relationship between the poet and the woman. It describes a game of tennis and subtly suggests the possibility of love between them. The fourth and final verse consists of the poet reflecting on what the woman might be doing now. It ends on an almost wistful note, suggesting loss and waste.

Paragraph 4

The poet uses a spare but concentrated diction to communicate the subdued emotions of the poem. He manages to suggest a lot through seemingly small details. For example, we learn that she, as a keen rider, jumps a fence she has already 'faltered at', *which, although metaphorical (she is hesitating whether to jump into marriage) suggests also her determination. In describing himself with her he uses the effective simile 'like an emblem of innocence and experience'. The alliteration of 'dismantled dreams' communicates the sense of her shattered hopes. The terse description of the accident that led to her first fiancé's death leads into the metaphorical description of her heart as 'untenanted, searching'. The question is posed: whether her concept of happiness as marriage to a 'good man' and looking after their home will ever be adequate as a substitute for the loss of first love.*

Paragraph 5

In the second verse, two effective similes create striking images in the reader's mind: the image of her potential new husband wading through the barley field 'like a fisherman in shallow seas' and his staring at the horizon

'as if a message were posted for his attention'.

The bleak terseness of the two words that end the verse ('saying nothing') suggests that his silence is ominous in some way.

Paragraph 6

The poet's ability to summon up an evocative image in brief phrases is represented by the opening of verse three 'Our game of tennis at dusk'. The image of 'our hands brushed lightly' is a small detail but it resonates, implying feelings between them that are left unspoken and not acted upon. 'The 'saying nothing' that ends the verse echoes the ending of the second verse.

Paragraph 7

In the final verse, the poet considers the two possibilities of her having married again and ruling 'a flagged kitchen' or living alone. The image 'do you trim the plant of a single life' uses a gardening metaphor to suggest a person who has retired from the world and finds satisfaction in the small pleasures of life. The image 'sheathed in a green glove' somehow suggests the protected retreat from life that she has settled for.

Closing paragraph

In a comparatively short poem, then, Nicholas Murray has managed to create a picture, through simile, metaphor and striking imagery, of a person's life and some of the relationships in it. The details he has chosen to represent the life of the 'tall girl' manage to build up an overall sense of loss and disappointment. He also manages to suggest the poet's own sense of regret about a 'lost love' or the possibility of love. The concentration and resonance of the diction leave the reader with an understanding of the life of 'the tall girl from Kildare'.

- Does the first paragraph function as an effective opening paragraph to the essay? Does it address the topic and say something specific, avoiding waffle?

- What do the second and third paragraphs attempt to do?

- Which specific poetic characteristics does the essay deal with in the next four paragraphs?

- How does the closing paragraph bring the essay back to the assignment as a whole and provides an effective ending?

10
SAMPLE ESSAY 5:
A MEDIA STUDIES ESSAY

• • • • • • • • • • • • • • • • •

A media studies essay involves you in analysing aspects of the mass media such as the press, films, television, the internet and other means of mass communication. One of the keys to writing successful essays on this subject area is detailed analysis. That means it is very important to back up general assertions about the media with relevant, specific examples. Media studies is often accused of encouraging superficial and 'waffly' writing, so indulge in some close detailed analysis to ward off that criticism.

Below is another sample essay written in response to this media or film studies assignment:

'The western film with its use of the myths and legends associated with the settlement of the American West has helped to shape America's view of itself.' Discuss.

Opening paragraph

There is no doubt that the western as a film genre is central to the way America sees itself and how Americans think of themselves. The settlement of the American West during the second half of the nineteenth century was a defining period in American history, around which many myths were created that have continued to shape American thinking right up to the present day. What it is to be an American citizen and the values embodied in that ideal have been shaped by the legends of the old west. The image of the intrepid pioneer heading off down the Oregon Trail to discover and tame the uncharted territory of the 'wild west' is deeply embedded in the American consciousness, however transformed American society has become in the century or so since the major migrations westwards took place. Western films represent some of these myths dearest to the heart of many American citizens.

Paragraph 2

Westerns, then, deal with the legends associated with the settlement of the western territories, but not necessarily, and not usually, with accurate historical facts. Myths are born not out of historical accuracy, but emerge from values and beliefs that grow round historical events. Yes, pioneers in their thousands poured westwards in search of land, gold or merely a fresh start in the vast open spaces of the western plains, but the struggles they endured during these long treks are generally portrayed in western films as consisting of battling hostile Native

Americans or 'bad guys' determined to rule the roost. The struggles these pioneers had were more to do with battling the elements, disease and hunger rather than fighting off 'savages' or lawless gunfighters. Yet movies such as 'The Searchers' and 'How the West Was Won' emphasise the conflict with 'Indians' because that is perceived as being more dramatic and appropriate for action movies, which western films are basically. This leads to a simplification of the issues involved in the settling of the west and the interaction with Native American tribes. At the heart of most western movies is the romanticised portrayal of the heroism of the pioneers who faced all these dangers to tame the new frontier.

Paragraph 3

However, it is only comparatively recently that western movies have faced the reality that some form of genocide was practised in relation to the Native American tribes when the west was settled by huge numbers of white settlers. Western movies have generally portrayed Native Americans as savage hordes standing in the way of inevitable progress. How many westerns have employed the image of the intrepid pioneers in a circle of wagons fighting off the brutal attacks of the 'Indians'? Nevertheless, some later westerns such as 'Little Big Man,' 'Soldier Blue' and 'Dances With Wolves' have tried to redress the balance and show the savagery that existed on both sides of the conflict. Yet the enduring myth that was nurtured by westerns and stayed in the American consciousness is that of the settlers taming the land despite the efforts of the tribes to massacre them.

Paragraph 4

Another central myth that the western movie preserves and encourages is that of the bringing of law and order to the lawless new territories by means of the gun and the skilled gunfighter. The role of the gun and the gunman are central to the western genre and in turn have helped to create a gun culture in American society with sometimes disastrous consequences. The 'fast gun', the hero who is 'fast on the draw', is the archetypal western hero. Sometimes he is a straightforward heroic type, in other films he is more complicated. The gunfighter uses his special skills to help the oppressed to establish law and order in communities where there has been none. In the western movie, 'Shane', for example, the hero is a professional gunfighter who is trying to leave gun-fighting behind him, but who is drawn back into his profession by his wish to help a community of homesteaders against a tyrannical cattle baron. At the end of the movie, the gunfighter leaves the community after defeating the bad guys because he knows there is no place for him in the community as the brand of the gunfighter will always stick to him. The film endorses the idea that the settlers' way of life has to be defended with the gun in the hands of a professional.

Paragraph 5

Such western heroes as Buffalo Bill, Billy the Kid, Wyatt Earp, Annie Oakley and Jesse James were first celebrated in the pages of cheap pulp fiction and then endlessly represented in western movies. These portrayals have little to do with their historical reality but are highly-romanticised versions of their lives, the purpose of which is to establish them as heroic figures of the old west. They become mythical archetypes around whom legends grow. The outlaw figures, such as Jesse James and Billy the Kid, are not mere criminals, but symbols of the lawless American west, romantic heroes who have been unjustly treated. The outlaw as a symbol of the west is part of the American consciousness and has helped to create the glamorisation of the criminal in American culture and life.

Closing paragraph

The western film, then, has inevitably perpetuated the myths of the American west. Western films are entertainment, but they also carry messages about America as a country that found its true identity through the settling of the west. In these films and the myths they propagate, historical reality becomes shrouded in myth. Unpalatable facts about the treatment of Native Americans are largely ignored or glossed over. Even though America's population has changed dramatically over the last decades, particularly with the growth in numbers of citizens with Hispanic origins, for many Americans the myths of the west as portrayed in western movies still hold sway and affect the way Americans think of themselves and their country.

Opening paragraph

- Does the first sentence address the essay topic and get the essay off to a brisk start?

- How do the next three sentences develop the point made in the first sentence? Are they 'meaty' and specific enough in their focus?

- How does the last sentence of the paragraph act as a summarising sentence?

Paragraph 2

- What linking word is used to connect the opening paragraph with the first paragraph of the body of the essay?

- How does the opening sentence signal to the reader that the second paragraph is to develop the theme of the first paragraph?

- What specific examples are used in sentences two to five to flesh out points made about the historical accuracy of western films?

- How does the last sentence act as a summarising and closing sentence to the paragraph?

Paragraph 3

- Which word acts as the linking word between paragraphs two and three?

- Does the first sentence of the paragraph act as the key sentence and if so, how?

- How do sentences two, three and four develop this key point?

- What specific examples are given?

- How does the last sentence act as a closing and summarising sentence to the paragraph?

Paragraph 4

- What is the linking word used in the first sentence?

- If the first sentence is the key sentence of the paragraph, what does it say the paragraph is to be about?

- How do sentences two, three and four develop this key point?

- Are they specific with detail?

- How do sentences five, six and seven provide detailed analysis to back up the key point of the paragraph?

Paragraph 5

- Which phrase acts as a linking phrase between paragraphs four and five? How does the first sentence act as the key sentence of the paragraph?

- How do sentences two, three and four develop this point?

- What specific examples are provided?

- How does the last sentence emphasise the key point and make a link between western heroes and another aspect of American culture?

Closing paragraph

- Which word indicates to the reader that this is the concluding paragraph of the essay?

- How does the first sentence reiterate the main point about western movies?

- How do sentences two to five round off the essay by emphasising the main points made in the essay but without slavish repetition?

11
SAMPLE ESSAY 6: HISTORY

● ● ● ● ● ●

The writing of 'history' essays involves following the same structured approach as in other subject areas. However, the 'evidence' you use to back up your analysis of historical events is clearly subject-specific. You need to know your 'facts' or relevant historical factors that have shaped important events and you must be able to select from the body of knowledge you have acquired to back up general assertions you are making in your essays. Just as in the sample literature essays, close references to the text and quotations were used to back up specific points, so in history essays detailed evidence and references to specific events have to be used to back up your analysis.

What were the origins of the First World War?

Opening paragraph

The catalyst that led to the outbreak of the First World War was the assassination of Archduke Franz Ferdinand, heir apparent to the Austrian-Hungarian empire, by a Serbian nationalist on June 24, 1914. A month later hostilities broke out, but Europe had been lurching towards a major war for a considerable time before that. The shooting of an obscure member of the Austrian aristocracy was merely the starting-gun for the war, not the central cause. The basic cause of the conflict was the rivalry between the major powers, Germany and its ally, Austria and its Austrian-Hungarian Empire, (known as the Central Powers) on the one side, and Britain, France and Russia (known as the Entente) on the other. The issues that divided these two power blocs were the balance of power in Europe as a whole, the search for colonial territories and the expansion of wealth and influence.

Paragraph 2

Britain, for example, wanted to maintain the balance of the power in Europe so that it could get on with governing and exploiting its huge world empire. The rise of any dominant power in Europe would threaten, in Britain's eyes, European stability and its own security. Germany was that power. The militaristic dictatorship, Kaiser Wilhelm II and the army, that was, in essence, in control of power in Germany, had been taking a more aggressive stance in the decades leading up to the outbreak of the war. From Britain's perspective, an over-dominant Germany would upset the natural balance in Europe and threaten its empire and even its own territorial integrity.

Paragraph 3

What, then, had Germany done specifically to arouse alarm bells in the rest of Europe? In the 1890s, it had rejected an alliance with Russia. Russia, governed by the almost feudal system of the Tsars, was alarmed by the bellicose stance of the Germans and in 1894, they signed an alliance with France. Russia had its own huge internal problems as demands for liberalisation grew and the feudal aristocracy that had ruled the country for centuries came under greater and greater pressure. The German rulers probably sensed that Russia was a very weakened state, especially after its 1905 defeat at the hands of the Japanese.

Paragraph 4

In addition, British alarm grew when Germany started to build up its navy. Traditionally, Britain prided itself on 'ruling the waves', the basis of its 'island fortress' reputation. Because of its sea power, Britain as an island power could protect its shores and patrol its huge empire. The method of diplomacy used to resolve conflicts in its empire was basically a 'send a gunboat' approach and this reliance on its naval power was still very much at the forefront of British policy, so that Germany's ambitions to build a navy that would at least rival Britain's was a like a red rag to the British bulldog. Not since Napoleon and the battle of Trafalgar had British sea power been seriously threatened and now Germany was doing just that.

Paragraph 5

Importantly, Germany had imperial ambitions as well, seeking to rival Britain in Africa especially. What Germany wanted from expanded colonial territories was similar to British expectations of its colonies: natural resources such as oil and gas, vital materials such as rubber and cotton, new markets for its own domestic goods and areas of the world where German capitalism could flourish in general. The Great War could be perceived as basically a war between two major competing imperial powers battling out in the trenches for the right to colonise and exploit. By the outbreak of the war, the Austrian-Hungarian Empire was already a crumbling edifice beset by strife caused by the aspirations of the subject peoples to self-determination. It had to ally itself with Germany in an attempt to prolong its existence. France, on the other hand, although a major imperial power, was relatively militarily weak in comparison with Britain and Germany. The war was essentially a contest for dominance between the two major imperial players, Britain and Germany.

Paragraph 6

Thus, when the Archduke Ferdinand was assassinated, Germany immediately backed Austria against the Serbs. With Russia allying itself with the Serbs, this brought Britain and France into play through the Entente. When Germany invaded neutral Belgium in order to attack France, Britain appeared to have no choice but to declare war against Germany. Not only was France an ally, Britain felt menaced by the Belgian ports being in German hands. War became inevitable and Europe became engulfed in a war that would devastate huge areas and result in the deaths of millions of people, end the rule of the German Kaisers, break up the Austrian-Hungarian Empire and redraw the map of Europe after the treaty of Versailles in 1919.

Closing paragraph

It can be seen, therefore, that the origins of the war were complex. At the heart of it, however, was the struggle for dominance between two major powers, a conflict that would erupt twenty years later when Hitler's Germany would seek to expand and establish a similar hegemony over Europe. Although Britain was the apparent victor of the First World War, the nature of British society was changed forever. No longer could the ruling classes expect the unquestioning support of the masses. With hindsight, it could be argued that the demise of the British Empire began in earnest after the First World War, although it would take another thirty years to unravel. It is ironic that it was the quest for colonial expansion that was one of the root causes of the war.

- How does the first sentence address the topic and get the essay off to a brisk start?

- How does the rest of the opening paragraph map out the ground that will be covered in the rest of the essay?

- What linking phrase is used in the first sentence of paragraph two?

- Does the first sentence of this paragraph act as the key sentence?

- How does the last sentence of this second paragraph emphasise the key point of the paragraph?

- Which word is used to provide a signpost between paragraphs two and three?

- How does the first sentence of the third paragraph act as the key sentence?

- How does the rest of this paragraph answer the question that has been asked in the opening sentence?

- Which phrase is used in the first sentence of the fourth paragraph to provide continuity?

- What does this first sentence indicate is the topic of the paragraph?

- Which word used in the opening sentence of the fifth paragraph acts as a link?

- How do the following sentences of the paragraph provide detail to flesh out the key point made in the first paragraph?

- How is the sixth paragraph linked to the previous paragraphs?

- What is the key point made in the opening sentence of the paragraph?

- How is that point developed in the remainder of the paragraph?

- Which word in the opening sentence of the closing paragraph indicates that a conclusion is about to be made?

- How does the concluding paragraph act as a summarising paragraph to the essay?

12
SAMPLE ESSAY 7: WRITING ABOUT A NOVEL

● ● ● ● ● ● ● ● ● ● ● ● ● ● ● ● ●

Writing an essay about a novel demands a slightly different approach from writing about a play or poetry. As with essays on plays, you must avoid paraphrasing or more or less telling the story ('plot' in terms of a play) of the novel. You must understand what aspects of the novel you are being asked to write about and concentrate on those, rather than retelling the whole story and commenting on characters who may be irrelevant to the assignment. You must, however, make close references to the novel, mentioning relevant incidents or things that relevant characters have said to back up the points you are trying to make. The opportunity to quote at any length are limited (unless you are writing a very long piece) so quotes should be brief and embedded at intervals in your essay rather than in big chunks of quotation.

Below is an essay written in response to the following topic:

'In "Great Expectations", Pip has to regain his moral values after losing them along the way.' Discuss this analysis of the novel.

Opening paragraph

Pip's values of kindness, industry, lack of pride and common humanity that he learnt from his childhood at the forge through the influence of Joe and Biddy, are gradually lost by him when he comes into his 'great expectations', leaves for London and enters the society world he aspires to. [1] The false values of Miss Havisham and Estella lead Pip into superficiality and snobbery, and a rejection of Joe and the honest, simple values the blacksmith stands for. It is his realisation that it is the convict he had rescued all those years ago on the marshes and not Miss Havisham who is his benefactor that brings him face to face with what kind of man he has become in London. [2] His moral journey is complete when he faces up to his responsibility for Magwitch and regains his moral values. [3]

Paragraph 2

We learn of Joe Gargery's influence on Pip in the opening chapters of the novel. [1] Joe is illiterate and finds it difficult to communicate his thoughts and feelings in words, but there is an innate gentleness and kindness to the man that Pip is very conscious of. For example, he tries his best to protect Pip from his sister who has brought him up 'by hand' and with frequent punishments from the 'tickler'. Joe and Pip have a natural understanding about Mrs Joe's 'rampages' and although the blacksmith is not strong enough to stand up to his wife, he tries his best to warn Pip of impending trouble. Equally, Joe is ill-at-ease when Uncle Pumblechook, Wopsle and Mr and Mrs Hubble dine with them because they are so full of petty snobberies, greed and pretensions. [2] He lacks the strength to assert himself in front of these absurd people, but he reaches an unspoken understanding with Pip about them. [3]

Paragraph 3

Furthermore, [1] *when Magwitch, the convict, apologises to Joe on the marshes for having stolen a dram of liquor and a pie from the smithy (Magwitch here is protecting Pip who has been responsible for taking them), Joe shows his natural sympathy and humanity by saying, 'we wouldn't have you starved to death for it, poor miserable fellow-creatur, would us, Pip?'* [2] *Pip learns a lesson here about showing kindness to the most wretched of human beings, a lesson he will in time forget and only remember when he has reached a low point in his own life. Pip feels his first feelings of guilt about Joe when he is unable to be honest with Joe about having stolen the file from the smithy.* [3] *This is the first real sign of a rift between the two, which will gradually increase to a chasm.* [4]

Paragraph 4

The next time [1] *Pip feels separate and ashamed of Joe occurs when the blacksmith accompanies Pip to Satis House so that Miss Havisham can reward Pip with twenty-five guineas.* [2] *Miss Havisham's imperious ways tie Joe's tongue into knots so that he is scarcely able to make any sense when he speaks. He also has trouble with his hat, a problem that will be echoed when he visits Pip in the London apartment he shares with Herbert Pocket. Pip feels guilt about how ashamed he is about Joe's lack of sophistication, but he cannot control his feelings. He has by now fallen in love with the cold and snobbish Estella, who with her mocking eyes disdains Joe's awkwardness and simplicity.* [3]

Paragraph 5

Biddy, too, [1] *signifies honesty and warmth in the novel.* [2] *Because he has fallen in love with Estella, Pip grows increasingly unhappy with his life at the forge and dreams of being a gentleman so that he can win Estella. He discusses his feelings with Biddy and clumsily states that he wishes he could fall in love with her rather than the proud Estella. 'But you never will, you see',* [3] *Biddy states, because she has the insight to understand that Pip has been smitten and that the life of the forge will never satisfy Pip now that Estella has told him how coarse and common he is. Biddy, by asking Pip whether he really thinks that becoming a gentleman will make him any happier, reveals her understanding of human nature.* [4]

Paragraph 6

When Pip comes into his expectations, believing Miss Havisham to be his benefactor, and he leaves for the life of a gentleman in London, the gap between Joe, Biddy and the forge, and the new Pip becomes huge. [1] *This is represented particularly in the chapter describing Joe's visit to Pip and Herbert's chambers. Firstly, Joe is dressed in formal clothes, which he finds most uncomfortable, especially the tight shirt collar he is wearing. He then has great difficulty in putting down his hat so that it does not topple over constantly. He addresses Pip as 'sir' and is clearly very ill-at-ease throughout the visit. Pip has arranged that Joe visit him in his chambers rather than at Hammersmith, because he knows Herbert will be sympathetic and because he does not want*

Bentley Drummle and Estella to encounter the awkward blacksmith. During Joe's visit, Pip becomes increasingly exasperated and embarrassed by Joe's gaucheness, a feeling that makes him feel ashamed but which he cannot control. At the end of the visit, Joe confesses that his trip has been a terrible mistake and that he was always ill-at-ease whenever he left the forge. [2] Joe's visit is a symbolic event in the alienation of Pip from his early years. Joe's statement about their being 'ever the best of friends' now rings hollowly. [3]

Paragraph 7

It is Bentley Drummle, indeed, [1] who symbolises the worst aspects of the London society to which Pip aspires to belong. [2] Drummle is cold, calculating, snobbish, proud and cruel, and it is no surprise when the equally cold Estella marries him eventually. Pip is Drummle's love rival and they both belong to the Finches, a club for young gentlemen. Because Pip feels he has to belong in this world, he begins to overspend and runs up huge debts. He has come a long way from being a penniless blacksmith's apprentice, but he is no happier for it. [3] He has by now lost touch with the values that had been forged in him through Joe and Biddy. [4]

Paragraph 8

The return of Magwitch, however, [1] forces Pip to face up to some realities. [2] Miss Havisham is not his anonymous benefactor, who turns out to be the convict he had helped all those years ago. This revelation is devastating to Pip, and all his illusions about his being the favoured protégé of Miss Havisham are shattered. Initially, he is full of horror at having to have dealings with the ex-convict and contemplates abandoning him. Gradually, however, he realises he owes this man a great deal and is touched by Magwitch's belief in his loyalty and gratitude. He does his best to protect him and decides that he must return to Australia with him; a plan that is thwarted at the last moment. [3] By assuming the mantle of responsibility for Magwitch, Pip regains the moral values he has lost. It is ironic that he is breaking the law in doing so, but Pip appears to acknowledge that there is a higher law he must obey, the law of common humanity. [4]

Paragraph 9

As a result of his debts, Pip is almost destitute and he has reached the lowest point of his life and falls gravely ill. [1] Joe and Biddy help to nurse him back to life, symbolising their forgiveness for his neglect and shabby treatment of them. Pip even contemplates marrying Biddy, but discovers that Joe and Biddy have married after Pip's sister dies. Part of Pip's regeneration process is that he has to leave the country and earn an honest living abroad before he returns to England, restored to health and having a purpose to his life. [2] He is reunited with Joe and Biddy, which symbolises his embrace of the values they stand for. Dickens decided to attach a happy ending to the novel with the implication that Estella and Pip will get married, but this is unconvincing. Estella has herself discarded her former false values, having discovered her own humble origins. [3]

Closing paragraph

Dickens, then, [1] has represented Pip's moral journey from honesty to dishonesty, lack of pride to snobbery, human warmth to emotional coldness, and back again. [2] The interesting aspect of Pip's journey is that we, as readers, cannot simply condemn him for his aspirations. We can understand his need to better himself, we can sympathise with his love for the disdainful Estella and even with his exasperation with Joe. In addition, Dickens makes us understand why Pip would be so horror-struck at the revelation that a convict was his benefactor. It is because Pip seems all too human in his failings that we can warm to the account of his moral journey and rejoice in his moral regeneration.

ANALYSIS

Opening paragraph

(1) The opening sentence of the essay addresses the topic immediately by mentioning the values that Pip has learnt at the forge and then contrasts them with those values he encounters in London. 'Waffle' is avoided because the first sentence says something specific about the novel.

(2) Sentences two and three provide further relevant response to the question by mentioning Miss Havisham and Estella and their influence on him. These are again specific references introducing subjects that will be dealt with later in the essay.

(3) The last sentence refers to the central topic of 'moral values' and makes mention of Magwitch and Pip's feelings of responsibility

towards him. This once again focuses on the central topic of the essay.

Paragraph 2

(1) Sentence one picks up on a point made in the opening paragraph (Joe Gargery's influence on Pip). This helps to establish the impression that you are going to follow up on the points you made in the first paragraph.

(2) Sentences two, three and four give detailed examples of Joe's attitudes with close references to the novel. Joe's attempts to protect Pip from his wife's 'rampages' and his dislike of the snobbery of the relatives are mentioned to illustrate the values Joe stands for.

(3) The last sentence makes a general statement about Joe that emphasises Joe's moral influence and ends the paragraph neatly.

Paragraph 3

(1) 'Furthermore,' is used as a linking word to provide continuity between this paragraph and the previous one. Note the comma after 'Furthermore'.

(2) A short quotation is used to back up the point that is being made. Note that it is contained within quotation marks. Short quotations from novels can be used to back up the point you are making, but don't overdo their use.

(3) Sentences two and three provide further detailed evidence (the point about Pip and the theft of the file from the smithy) to back up the main point of the paragraph.

(4) Sentence four summarises the paragraph and makes the point about the rift between Joe and Pip.

Paragraph 4

(1) The phrase 'The next time' acts as a linking phrase between paragraphs.

(2) The opening sentence tells the reader what this paragraph is to be about: the beginnings of Pip's move away from the values of the forge to his embracing the values of Satis House.

(3) Sentences two, three and four 'flesh out' the key point with detailed references to his feeling ashamed of Joe and his reactions to the scorn of Estella.

Paragraph 5

(1) 'too' is used as a linking word between paragraphs.

(2) Sentence one is the key sentence indicating that the subject of the paragraph is Biddy and her influence.

(3) Another short quotation is used (within quotation marks) which adds relevant detail to the topic of the sentence.

(4) The closing sentence of the paragraph makes a general statement about Biddy that 'ties up' the paragraph neatly.

Paragraph 6

(1) Sentence one acts as the key sentence to the paragraph by mapping out what the rest of the paragraph is to deal with: the impact Pip's inheritance has on his relationship with Joe and the forge.

(2) Sentences two to six provide plenty of detail and close references to Joe's visiting Pip in London and illustrate the key point of the paragraph.

(3) The last sentence acts as a summarising sentence to the paragraph by emphasising the break between Pip and his old life.

Paragraph 7

(1) 'indeed' is the linking word used to link the paragraphs.

(2) Sentence one is the key sentence indicating that Bentley Drummle and the world he represents are the topics of the paragraph.

(3) Sentences two, three and four add relevant detail by references to Drummle, Estella and the Finches. These references back up the point about the kind of values Drummle stands for, which seem to be influencing Pip.

(4) The last sentence draws a general conclusion about Pip's loss of values based on the points discussed in the paragraph.

Paragraph 8

(1) ' however' is used a linking word.

(2) Sentence one indicates the key point of the paragraph is the return of Magwitch.

(3) Sentences two to six add detailed references to back up the key point by analysing Pip's changing attitudes to Magwitch.

(4) The last two sentences of the paragraph both emphasise the general point that can be deduced from the points that have been made.

Paragraph 9

(1) Sentence one is the key sentence of the paragraph by mentioning Pip's descent into illness and depression.

(2) Sentences two, three, four and five develop this main point by referring to Joe and Biddy's kindness and Pip's gradual regeneration.

(3) The last two sentences add additional value to the paragraph by making a judgement about the ending of the novel with reference to the possible marriage of Estella and Pip.

Closing paragraph

(1) 'then' indicates that a conclusion is about to be reached.

(2) Sentence one brings the essay back to the overall assignment you have been set.

(3) The rest of the paragraph leaves the reader with something to think about and inserts a personal response to the question that has been set.

13

SAMPLE ESSAY 8:
WRITING IN RESPONSE TO A
CRITICAL THINKING TASK

● ● ● ● ● ● ● ● ● ● ● ● ● ● ● ● ● ●

Critical thinking involves close textual analysis and evaluation of arguments. You will be expected to identify in the given text how the argument is structured, the conclusions that are drawn from the points that are being made and any counter-arguments that are presented. You are expected to display your understanding of the assumptions that underpin arguments and to analyse any flaws in the argument.

You are not usually asked to write a complete essay in response to the assignment, but a shorter, detailed piece of continuous writing.

Assignment: Write a critical evaluation of the argument presented below. Ensure that in your answer you:

1) Explicitly identify the structure of the argument, that is, conclusions drawn, reasons given, and counter-assertions made. [5]

2) Assess the argument by explaining the flaws in the reasoning, and giving the assumptions that must be made. [6]

3) Present two further arguments that challenge and/or support the conclusion. [6]

(Three marks are available for quality of written communication)

Global warming, its dangers for the planet and the reasons for it, has become something of a sacred cause for many environmental activists and some in the scientific community. However, the case that these advocates make for urgent action is often over-stated and flawed in the evidence that is presented. The situation is much less clear-cut than these zealots would claim. There may well be a case for accepting that the earth is warming, but even that is not a total certainty. At any rate, it must be remembered that the earth has always undergone climactic change independent of human interventions.

Extravagant claims were being made only a few years ago that within fifty years time, the average temperature of the globe would rise by an average of ten degrees. These wildly apocalyptic forecasts were being made by scientists and activists who stated that widespread ecological disaster awaited the planet and this was largely due to the impact of human behaviour through carbon emissions, the swallowing up of the earth's natural resources and pollution in general. This simply has not happened and those forecasts can now be seen as simply alarmist. Now it is generally agreed that those wild forecasts of doom were wholly exaggerated and that the effect of global warming, if it is to happen, would be far less drastic than was previously thought.

If those dire prognostications were false, what can be trusted in the current propaganda circulated through the media by those with a particular ecological axe to grind? The scientific evidence for global warming is, at best, contradictory. There have been many dissenting voices in the scientific community who doubt the very basis of the ecologist argument. Professor Otis Jones of Duke University, Illinois, for example, has claimed that the panic over global warming has been politically motivated. Yes, other scientists say, there may well be a process of global warming taking place, but the extent of it is much less dramatic that has been described hitherto. Perhaps some ice caps are melting, these scientists argue, but at such a slow rate that the planet is in no real danger. Yes, industry and cars are sources of carbon emissions, but no more than trees, which most ecologist activists would seek to protect.

The picture is confused and the problem is that one side of the argument seems to have a vested interest in keeping it that way by supplying half-truths and relying on half-baked scientific evidence. There has been an attempt to stampede the major industrial nations, especially the United States, into taking drastic action to cut emissions, an action that could seriously harm the country's economy and as a result, the world's. What is needed is a plain, common sense policy, not hysterical arguments. The available evidence, unless it is tainted by special interest groups, must be examined scientifically and unemotionally to find out exactly what the situation is. It may well be that the planet is warming and that that will have an effect on how we inhabit this earth. However, let us deal with facts, not fantasy, and apply our intelligence to the problem, if problem it be, and not our prejudices.

1. In the first paragraph, two intermediate conclusions are made: that the case for global warming has been exaggerated and that the situation is more confused than is often represented by the proponents of urgent action being taken on the issue. The counter-assertion is made that the earth has always undergone climate change, implying that there is nothing new about the current situation. The last sentence of the second paragraph concludes that recent forecasts about the impact of global warming have been inaccurate. The reasons that this conclusion is based on are that those scientists who made those predictions have had to water down their warnings because the disasters have not happened. In the third paragraph, the conclusion is made that the earth may well be warming, but the impact of this is less severe than has been claimed. Having admitted global warming may be happening, the writer gives some specific examples of the impact on the environment that help back up this conclusion. The final sentence of the article draws the conclusion that facts, and not fantasy, must be the basis for discussion of this issue. This conclusion is based on the opinions expressed in the preceding sentences of the paragraph that stress the emotional, irrational nature of the arguments used to force action on global warming.

2. The main flaws are that there is 'lack of hard evidence to back up the argument and that it depends on rather empty assertions of the very kind that he/she accuses the other side of indulging in. In essence, the writer has provided little or no evidence for the opinions expressed. The arguments of those advocating urgent action are presented as born out of prejudice. The use of terms such as 'sacred cause', 'zealots', 'apocalyptic forecasts' and 'dire prognostications' are intended to create the impression that these people have allowed the intensity of their feelings to cloud their judgement, which leads them into presenting, at best, very partial evidence.

An assumption is made in the article that previous forecasts about global warming have been proved to be badly wrong, but no concrete examples to back up this point are provided. The statement that the earth has always been subject to climactic change implies the assumption that the planet has faced similar challenges in the past and has survived them and yet, once again, no specific examples are given. It is assumed that there are 'many dissenting voices in the scientific community', but this is only backed up by reference to one individual professor and 'others'.

The opinions the writer quotes these 'voices' as expressing are insufficiently detailed to stand up to any close scrutiny. The example of trees emitting carbon dioxide underlines an assumption, or, at least an inference, that 'zealots' would care more about trees than human activities.

The writer makes empty assertions about depending on hard, scientific facts rather than fantasy, but does not define what is meant by facts. Evidence must be examined but not evidence that is 'tainted by special interest groups'. Here the writer reveals once again his/her partial attitudes. Overall, the predominant tone of the piece is polemical rather than objective. In arguing for a common sense attitude to this issue, the writer is aiming to identify potential opponents as depending on the opposite of common sense. Common sense is in itself a fairly meaningless phrase in this context.

3. There is considerable evidence that global warming is having a serious impact on the planet. Recent ecological disasters such as the Tsunami in South-East Asia and the major floods in the southern states of the USA cannot just be dismissed as arbitrary acts of nature. The increasing frequency with which these abnormal events are taking place demonstrates clearly that something drastic and dangerous is happening on the planet. The vast preponderance of scientific opinion is now weighted towards acknowledging the serious crisis that the planet faces unless drastic action is quickly taken. Dissenting voices within the scientific community are becoming fewer and fewer.

The most significant evidence supporting the case for

drastic action is that most of the world's nations, large and small, now acknowledge the danger and that something must be done quickly. The fact that America, India and China, among other nations, are dragging their feet about taking effective action to reduce carbon omissions only highlights the threat to the world. These countries are sacrificing the future health of the planet for the sake of their own short-term and narrow economic interests. However, in the longer term, these nations will suffer with the rest of the world when the full effects of global warming impact. Droughts, floods, freak storms and widespread famine and disease will ultimately affect every country, whatever its size and state of development.

ANALYSIS

Answer to question 1

The answer specifically deals with the intermediate conclusions drawn and counter-assertions made in the given text and refers to the relevant sections. The reasons for the intermediate conclusions are analysed and specific examples given. The final conclusion that is drawn is identified and the reasons for the conclusion.

Answer to question 2

The flaws in the argument are stated as being lack of hard evidence and empty assertions without back-up evidence. The counter-arguments are characterised as prejudiced and using emotional language. It is pointed out that there are many dissenting voices but only one scientist is referred to. The analysis pinpoints the assumption that environmentalists care more about trees than human beings. Overall, the judgement is made that the piece is very partial and polemical rather than objective.

Answer to question 3

Specific details of ecological disasters are given to assert that global warming is a definite threat to the planet. An assertion is made about the majority of scientific opinion backing that analysis. In addition, an argument is made that almost all nations now acknowledge the danger, although some of the larger nations are dragging their feet in doing something about reducing emissions. Specific examples of the effect of global warming are presented to back the argument that is being made.

USEFUL WORDS AND PHRASES FOR USE IN CRITICAL THINKING TASKS

argument	drawing an analogy	making an assumption	bias	conclusion
conflict	consistency	context	corroboration	counter-argument
credibility	criterion	data	definition	dilemma
evidence	expertise	hypothetical	inference	inconsistency
intermediate conclusion	interpretation	irrelevant	judgement	language
neutrality	perception	principles	relevance	reputation
vested				

14

SAMPLE ESSAY 9: A FILM STUDIES ESSAY

An essay on film studies is different from essays on literature in that you cannot quote directly from a film. A quotation from a film would mean showing an extract from the film itself. You can, however, describe a relevant scene or shot and refer to particular movies to back up the points you are making. Film studies are particularly prone to the use of 'jargon', but nevertheless it is important to be able to discuss films using generally-accepted terminology within the subject area. It is therefore essential that you familiarise yourself with these terms and are able to use them with confidence.

Assignment: Explain the 'auteur theory' in film criticism and make a case for or against it, using examples of particular film directors.

Opening paragraph

The auteur theory [1] *originated in France in the 1950s in the pages of the 'Cahiers du Cinema', a journal of serious film criticism for whom critics such as Jean-Luc Godard, Claude Chabrol and Francois Truffaut, all of whom would later become distinguished directors themselves, wrote.* [2] *The magazine concentrated on the American film industry and their admiration for the Hollywood* film, especially genre movies such as westerns, thrillers and musicals. The French critics lavished praise on individual American directors such as Howard Hawks, Orson Welles, John Ford and Vincente Minnelli [3] who worked within the Hollywood industry but who managed, it was claimed, to impose a personal vision in the genre movies they directed. [4]

Paragraph 2

This, then, [1] was the basis of the auteur theory. The director became the 'author' of the film, just as the novelist was the author of the novel or a painter was the creator behind a work of art. Indeed, according to the critics who proposed the theory, the greatest directors were artists in their own right, despite the fact that they were working in an industrialised art form aiming to create product for a mass world-wide audience. Perhaps the major studios of Hollywood were operated like factories, churning out film after film to fill the programmes of the thousands of cinemas that needed their product, but individual 'geniuses', such as those mentioned above and others that included Alfred Hitchcock, Samuel Fuller, Otto Preminger, George Stevens and Robert Aldrich, could manipulate the studio system to impose their own vision on the raw material they were presented with. [2] The making of a film might well be a collaborative exercise involving the talents of screenwriters, actors, cameramen, composers and all kinds of technicians, but to the proponents of the auteur theory, there was only one guiding genius: the director. [3] If the director was a mediocrity, then the film would be mediocre. If the director, however,

116

was one of the chosen geniuses, then the film had every chance of turning out to be a masterpiece. [4]

Paragraph 3

It can safely be asserted [1] *that the auteur theory arose partly out of the need of these French critics to promote the role of the director for their own personal reasons.* [2] *After all, when they were writing as critics, they were frustrated directors. They wanted to direct films themselves and by establishing their critical reputations via their advocacy of the auteur theory, they were making names for themselves in the film world and convincing people that the creation of worthwhile films depended on the overall vision of individual directors, which they fervently hoped to become themselves. Thus, the case that they made for individual Hollywood directors to be taken seriously as artists was exaggerated in the claims made for these 'geniuses'.* [3] *Indeed, it came as a great surprise to many of these directors that they had any kind of 'universal vision' and underlying themes that linked all their movies. Vincente Minnelli, for example, the talented director of musicals such as 'Meet Me in St Louis' and 'The Band Wagon' found himself elevated to auteur stature because these critics, unlike the rest of us, could discern the 'philosophy' that underpinned the movies he directed.* [4]

Paragraph 4

Thus, [1] *the auteur theory flew in the face of the hard facts of the Hollywood industry.* [2] *Directors were employees, employed, by and large, to turn a screenplay, which most often they had had no hand in creating, into celluloid. A contracted Hollywood director would be handed a script, actors would be cast, a cameraman and other technicians assigned, a shooting schedule worked out, and he (the vast majority of Hollywood directors were male) was expected to make the movie within the budget and on time for release. Very few directors had rights even over the final editing of the movies 'they' made. The studio heads would make these decisions guided by their own instincts and audience reactions to the sneak previews of the movie. The commercial potential of any movie was the most important factor for the studios. The pressure on the studio heads was to create box-office successes, not works of art.* [3] *If by accident a successful film in box-office terms was praised as being artistic, then that was just a happy accident.* [4]

Paragraph 5

However, [1] *talented directors did work within the Hollywood system and did manage to impose themselves on the material they worked on.* [2] *Alfred Hitchcock, for example, made 'thriller' movies that could fairly be claimed to be works of art. Movies such as 'Vertigo', 'Psycho', 'North By Northwest' and 'Notorious' are entertaining genre films, but they are also worthy of serious consideration. However, Hitchcock did not make these movies by himself. He was very astute at picking talented collaborators without whom the movies would have been much less impressive. Try to think of the best of Hitchcock's movies without the scores of Bernard Herrmann, for example, or the cinematography of Robert Burks ('Vertigo', 'North by Northwest').* (3) *Film-making is a collaborative process and even the ablest of directors cannot do everything themselves.* (4)

Paragraph 6

Nevertheless, (1) *some directors acquired more control over the films they made by becoming independent producers and working out deals with the major studios.* (2) *When a producer/director has control over casting, script, editing and almost all the other aspects of film-making, then he or she can make a claim to some kind of authorship, but even then they are dependent on the artistic input of many people: actors, cinematographers, screenwriters, production designers, among many others.* (3) *Ingmar Bergman, the great Swedish director, had as much control over the films he directed as any director who ever worked in the cinema, but even he needed the talents of cinematographers and actors to get his vision onto the screen.* (4)

Closing paragraph

Thus, (1) *the central flaw in the auteur theory is this need to identify the director as the sole presiding genius over the creation of a film.* (2) *A novelist can write alone, creating a novel from the raw material he/she provides. A film director, working in the commercial world of the film industry, can never work alone. Any film is the sum total of all the talents that contributed to it. The critics who first pushed the auteur theory were intent on raising the profile of film directors per se and they were successful in doing this. However, they made exaggerated claims for many individual directors, claims which only the most diehard of auteurists would now endorse.* [3] *The auteur theory was flawed from the beginning and as structuralist and post-structuralist theory has revealed the commonality of all artistic endeavour, it can be granted even less critical credence than before.* [4]

Analysis

Opening paragraph

(1) Using the term 'auteur theory' as the opening words of the essay signals to the reader that you are addressing the topic immediately.

(2) This is an emphatic opening sentence saying something specific about the subject by explaining how the theory arose and mentioning some of the leading supporters of auteurism. 'Waffle' is avoided.

(3) Specific examples of directors favoured by the auteur critics are provided, but no detail is gone into at this stage of the essay.

(4) This last sentence of the opening paragraph points the way for what is to come in the body of the essay.

Paragraph 2

(1) 'This' refers back to the opening paragraph and provides a link, as does 'then'.

(2) This long sentence explains further the thinking behind the theory and details particular directors favoured by the supporters of the theory.

(3) This sentence acknowledges the collaborative nature of film-making but emphasises the centrality of the role of the director, according to the auteur theory.

(4) The final two sentences of the paragraph are a neat expression of the gist of what has been stated.

Paragraph 3

(1) 'It can safely be asserted' acts as a linking device.

(2) The first sentence of the paragraph makes the key point of the paragraph that the supporters of the auteur theory had something personal to gain from proposing it.

(3) Sentences two, three and four develop this key point further.

(4) The last two sentences present a specific example of a director and draw a conclusion from what has been stated.

Paragraph 4

(1) 'Thus' is used as a linking word between paragraphs.

(2) The first sentence of the paragraph clearly states the subject of the paragraph (the industrial nature of Hollywood film-making) in a clear, simple sentence.

(3) Sentences two to six develop this point, providing detail of what the role of director was expected to be within the Hollywood industry.

(4) The last sentence adds an additional idea about films of merit made within this system being a 'happy accident', which rounds off the paragraph.

Paragraph 5

(1) 'However' is the linking word between paragraphs.

(2) The first sentence clearly states that the topic of the paragraph is about how some directors manage to impose a personal vision on the films they direct.

(3) Sentences two to five examine the work of one director in particular, Alfred Hitchcock, to illustrate the point. Specific films directed by Hitchcock are referred to.

(4) The last sentence makes a counter-assertion about Hitchcock's movies, which refers back to the point about film-making as a collaborative process.

Paragraph 6

(1) 'Nevertheless' is the linking word between paragraphs.

(2) The topic of the paragraph (directors acting as their own producers) is stated in the first sentence of the paragraph.

(3) The long second sentence details some of the functions of the producer, but reiterates the idea that film-making is a collaborative process.

(4) The last sentence uses the example of an individual director to emphasise this point.

Closing paragraph

(1) 'Thus' signals to the reader that the essay is coming to a considered conclusion based on the arguments made in the body of the essay.

(2) The first sentence reiterates the central argument about the flaws in the auteur theory.

(3) Sentences two to six summarise the arguments against the auteur theory.

(4) The last sentence leaves the reader with something else to think about: the influence of recent critical theory on our attitude to auteurism.

15

SAMPLE ESSAY 10:
A POLITICS ESSAY

● ● ● ● ● ● ● ● ● ● ● ● ●

Writing essays about politics and political history clearly shares common ground with history essays. You have to have your facts at your fingertips and familiarise yourself with the accepted terms of the subject area. Your close analysis has to be backed up with relevant and specific examples that illustrate the points you are making.

Assignment: What factors led to the landslide victory for the British Labour Party in the 1945 election?

Opening paragraph

The landslide victory of the Labour Party in the 1945 election was one of the biggest upsets in British electoral history. [1] *The Conservative Party, under the leadership of the then Prime Minister Winston Churchill, had confidently expected a return to power after the wartime coalition with Labour, but their defeat at the polls was not only a rejection of Churchill as the man to lead Britain in peace-time and during a period of inevitable major reconstruction, but also of their pre-war record as a government. The overall Labour majority was 145 seats, a huge margin, and a testimony to the fact that voters, by and large, wanted a fresh start and not a return to the policies that had caused so much social misery in the 1930s.* [2]

Paragraph 2

The experience of the majority of the British people during the 1930s was undoubtedly [1] *a major factor in giving their votes to the Labour Party.* [2] *The Great Depression of the 1930s, after the Wall Street crash of 1929, had led to mass unemployment in Britain. With minimal social security available to the mass of the population, the working classes endured years of deprivation and struggle to meet the very basic needs of food, housing and health care. There was no safety net for the mass of the population to fall back onto. Millions lived in wretched city slums and were seriously undernourished. The lack of nutritious food meant many children and old people, in particular, suffered from ill-health. Free medical care was very scarce and when the choice was between putting food on the table or paying the doctor's bills, millions had to choose the survival route and neglect basic health needs.* [3] *And who was in charge during this decade of social deprivation? The Conservatives, who were now asking the people who had endured under their government of the 1930s to give them once again their trust. The bitter experience of that decade, however, had not been forgotten and it would cost the Tory Party dearly.* [4]

Paragraph 3

It must also be stressed [1] that the 1945 election was the first opportunity the electorate had had to choose their government since 1935. [2] When war broke out in 1939, elections were suspended so the British people had had no chance to register their approval or otherwise of government policies for ten whole years. Victory in Europe had been achieved with the surrender of Germany and its allies, but the war in the Pacific had still to be won. Most people acknowledged that Churchill had proved himself a great leader in wartime conditions. He became a symbol of British resistance to the Nazi war machine. However, voters had long memories and Churchill was associated in the nation's consciousness with the horrors of the 1930s. [3] Older voters, too, recalled the aftermath of the First World War ('the war to end all wars'), when promises about a reordering of British society had been made and then power and wealth had returned to the same people as before the war. In July 1945, as the war neared its close, the mass of the voters seemed determined that this time things would be very different. [4]

Paragraph 4

Another [1] important factor in the 1945 election was the widespread feeling among the population that they had made sacrifices to win the war and deserved some reward for those sacrifices. [2] Millions of men and women had served, and were still serving, in the armed forces. Almost a million people had made the ultimate sacrifice. Indeed, the votes of the serving soldiers were a decisive factor in making *sure Labour were returned to power with such a huge majority. Conscripted men and women had been separated from their families and given up their paid employment to serve their country.* [3] *They believed they deserved something better than what had faced them in the 1930s.* [4]

Paragraph 5

The wartime government under Churchill had, however, [1] *anticipated the restructuring of British society post-war and had produced the Beveridge Report, which had important recommendations about health, employment, social security and educational opportunities.* [2] *In the light of that report, the 1945 election manifestos of the two main parties make an interesting contrast. The Tory Party headed their manifesto 'Mr Churchill's Declaration of Policy to Electors', which made clear that they put great faith in the vote-winning capacity of the revered war leader. The manifesto stressed the need to push towards final victory and the reconstruction of Europe. It was less detailed about the kind of Britain the Party wanted to construct in post-war Britain. The Labour Party manifesto, by contrast, was heavily skewed towards the Beveridge Report and made very specific promises about establishing a welfare state in which the citizen would be cared for 'from the cradle to the grave'. There were pledges to nationalise key industries and utilities. A National Health Service, free to all citizens, was at the core of their plans.* [3] *The general impression was created that the Labour Party would be better able to rebuild British society with greater fairness, equality and opportunity.* [4]

Paragraph 6

In addition, [1] leading Labour politicians because of their prominent roles in the wartime coalition government had become very well-known to, and trusted by, the British electorate. [2] Clement Attlee, Ernest Bevin and Herbert Morrison, among others, were now perceived as capable politicians to whom the reins of government could now be safely entrusted. By contrast, Churchill was now in his seventies and seemed to many to belong to the past. Furthermore, Churchill made a grave error by stating that to implement the Labour Party programme would mean the creation of a Gestapo-like society. As the population had just been heavily involved in defeating the Gestapo and the totalitarian forces that had led Germany to defeat, this rebounded on Churchill and he was roundly criticised for the allusion. [3] In the election campaign, then, the Tory Party scored some own goals, while the Labour Party captured the mood of the nation. [4]

Closing paragraph

It was, then, [1] the widespread wish for a new beginning and a rejection of the policies of the 1930s that helped to win the Labour Party such an overwhelming victory in the 1945 election. The wartime experience of millions of ordinary people in the armed forces had reinforced their determination not to return to the kind of society they had endured pre-war. Additionally, the civilian population had suffered family dislocation and loss, blackouts, air raids, rationing, restriction of movement, and many other problems and the

majority of the voters wanted relief from those hardships in the post-war British society. The Labour Party with its promises about a kind of 'new deal' and a caring State that would intervene on behalf of the ordinary citizen against the old oligarchies and wealth-owners caught the mood of the people. (2)
The result was the landslide majority gifted to the Party by the voters. (3)

ANALYSIS

Opening paragraph

(1) The first sentence immediately addresses the topic of the assignment, the landslide 1945 victory, and says something specific about it.

(2) The long sentences two and three put the election into historical context by mentioning Churchill and the Conservative Party, his wartime leadership and the expectations of victory. The actual result of the election is then referred to.

Paragraph 2

(1) The use of 'undoubtedly' emphasises the point already made in the opening paragraph and acts as a linking word.

(2) The first sentence indicates what the paragraph is to be about: the experience of the British people in the 1930s.

(3) Sentences two to seven supply detailed examples of the hardships of the 1930s, citing historical events, mass unemployment, resultant poverty and the lack of state action to redress the hardships.

(4) The last three sentences draw an intermediate conclusion from the facts supplied in the paragraph, namely that the electorate held the Conservative Party responsible for the ills of the Depression.

Paragraph 3

(1) The words 'It must also be stressed' act as a linking device between this paragraph and previous one.

(2) This is the key sentence of the paragraph mentioning the 1945 election as the electorate's opportunity to pass a verdict on the pre-war government.

(3) Sentences two to seven develop this key point, emphasising the electorate made a distinction between Churchill's role as a successful war leader and the pre-war record of the Tories.

(4) The last two sentences make a point about older voters and reiterates the point about their desire to leave the past behind them and look to a better future.

Paragraph 4

(1) 'Another' serves as a linking word between paragraphs.

(2) The first sentence indicates to the reader what the paragraph is about: the belief among the electorate that they deserved some reward for having made sacrifices during the war.

(3) Sentences two, three and four expand on this point, mentioning the experience of men and women who had been in the armed forces.

(4) The final sentence is an emphatic reiteration of the key point.

Paragraph 5

(1) 'however' acts as a linking word between paragraphs.

(2) The first sentence mentions the key point of the Beveridge Report, which will be developed in the remainder of the paragraph.

(3) Sentences three to nine give plenty of detail in relation to the party manifestos and the Report.

(4) The last sentence draws a conclusion based on the statements made in the paragraph.

Paragraph 6

(1) 'In addition' is used as a linking device between paragraphs.

(2) The first sentence makes a point about the leading Labour politicians and acts as the key sentence of the paragraph.

(3) Sentences two to five develop that point by mentioning leading Labour politicians. A contrast is made with Churchill and a specific example is given of mistakes made by Churchill during the campaign.

(4) The last sentence of the paragraph draws a conclusion based on the statements made that the Labour Party ran a better campaign than the Tories.

Closing paragraph

(1) 'then' signals to the reader that a conclusion to the essay is being reached.

(2) Sentences one to four act as a final summing-up of the arguments made in the essay by detailing the main areas of dissatisfaction of the electorate.

(3) The final sentence neatly rounds off the essay by bringing the essay back to the landslide victory in the election.

16
GRAMMAR AND ACCURACY

● ● ● ● ● ● ● ● ● ● ● ● ● ● ● ● ● ● ●

Writing essays in a structured and clear way so that your reader/assessor can follow what you are trying to say is a very important factor in the assessment grade you achieve. Another important factor is the accuracy of what you write. By accuracy, we mean not only the clarity of the expression but the correctness of usage in terms of grammar, punctuation and spelling. If you make too many grammatical, punctuation and spelling errors in your writing, this will create the wrong impression and lose you marks so that your grade assessment will be affected.

Anyone, and that includes the author of this book and your teachers and assessors, can make grammatical, punctuation or spelling errors, especially when writing at speed, such as in an examination. The trick is to minimise these. The occasional error can be overlooked, but a multitude of them cannot. Examiners are usually told to penalise candidates whose writing is error-prone. That is true for coursework assignments as well as examinations. Indeed, as spell-checks and grammar checks are readily available on computers now, there is even less excuse to present flawed work for coursework.

In this section, we will look at some crucial areas where accuracy will pay dividends.

WRITING IN SENTENCES

Consider the following.

1. I am.

2. Because the voters turned against the party.

3. Making the reasons for the war very clear indeed.

4. Judges must be independent of government so that they can make decisions free of political influence.

5. Although efforts were made to patch up the quarrel.

6. The country declared war on the day after the invasion.

Three of the above are complete sentences and three are not. Sentences one, four and six are complete sentences because they make sense on their own.

Examples two, three and five are incomplete sentences because they clearly do not make sense standing on their own.

Example two could be an answer in speech to a question, but it would not be appropriate to use an incomplete sentence like this in an essay.

Example three, similarly, could be a comment as a response to something that has been said.

Example four lacks a main statement and is only a clause, not a complete sentence.

You must be able to write in complete sentences in formal essays. If you have any doubt about a sentence you have written, read it over 'in your head' and judge from the sense whether it is complete or not.

THE CONSTRUCTION OF SENTENCES

Read the following paragraph:

The government's reforms in education have definitely run into trouble. Not only are the opposition parties against them, but a substantial proportion of its own supporters are also up in arms at the proposals that were put forward in the recent White Paper. Many MPs fear that selection is being introduced via the back door and that the government's ultimate aim is the privatisation of education itself, which would be anathema to the bulk of the party. Whilst the main opposition party will go along with the main thrust of the government's reforms, they are arguing that they do not go far enough. Thus, the government is harangued from all sides.

The paragraph consists of five sentences: there are two short sentences and three longer sentences.

The short sentences come at the start and end of the paragraph. Is there a reason for this? Consider the first sentence:

The government's reforms in education have definitely run into trouble.

Because this is the key sentence of the paragraph, it makes a statement concisely and without further development. This kind of sentence is called a simple sentence. It has one main clause and makes one statement.

Sentences two, three and four, however, are more complex, because they elaborate on the points they are making:

Not only are the opposition parties against them but a substantial proportion of its own supporters are also up in arms at the proposals that were put forward in the recent White Paper.

This is an example of a complex sentence, because it has more than one clause and makes more than one statement. Sentences three, four and five are also complex sentences.

However, the last sentence of the paragraph is another simple sentence because one statement is made. That suits the function of this last sentence: it acts as a kind of summarising sentence for the paragraph.

The length and complexity of your sentences will depend on what you are trying to say in them. If you want to make an emphatic point in a clear and concise way, then a simple sentence is best:

Africa is facing a famine crisis.

However, if you want to elaborate on a point and analyse in detail, a complex sentence is more appropriate:

Aid agencies differ in their analysis of the situation because they put different emphases on various factors such as government corruption, civil wars, climate change, economic development and accessibility, but they all agree that a catastrophe is looming which the developed nations cannot ignore.

In this sentence, the main point made in the first section is developed in detail in the remainder of the sentence. It is appropriate that a complex sentence is employed.

In your essays, you should aim to use a variety of sentence structures and lengths. Frequently, it will be appropriate to use concise, simple sentences that make an emphatic point. However, when you want to expand on a point and analyse in greater detail, longer, complex sentences are appropriate.

One thing to avoid is writing in a succession of monotonous simple sentences. Consider this paragraph:

136

Fashion models nowadays achieve an amazing level of fame and income. Many people wonder why this is so. Models only parade on a catwalk. They wear designer clothes. They are not much more than clothes-horses. Yet they earn huge sums of money. They are an integral part of the celebrity culture of the present day.

This is all rather 'staccato' in style and rather monotonous. Look at this rewriting:

Fashion models nowadays achieve an amazing level of fame and income. Many people wonder why this is so because, after all, they only parade on a catwalk and wear designer clothes, which makes them not much more than clothes-horses. Yet they earn huge sums of money because they are an integral part of the celebrity culture of the present day.

The seven simple sentences of the first version become one simple sentence and two complex sentences in the improved second version. There is more flow in this version and more of a sense of developed thought, which arises partly because of the use of complex sentences.

In essays write in complete sentences. Vary the length and type of sentences you use according to what you are trying to do: making concise statements or analysing in detail.

PRACTICE (ANSWERS ON PAGE 157)

Below are two paragraphs, each consisting of six sentences. Rewrite them using one simple sentence and two complex sentences.

a) Women, on average, earn 30% less than men. Government

legislation under the Equal Pay Act has obviously not had the desired effect. It is a change in fundamental attitudes that is required. Government may have to use compulsion to equalise pay between the sexes. Economic disadvantage does not help the cause of women's rights. These are supposed to be at the heart of government policy.

b) The majority of film producers are hoping to make the ultimate blockbuster. This means that most films have a sameness about them. They are full of special effects, very loud soundtracks and juvenile content. A large potential audience exists for more intelligent cinema. Film-makers should not underestimate the taste of their audiences. At some point, audiences will tire of no-brainer movies.

PUNCTUATION

All sentences start with a capital letter and end with a full stop. Of course, you have to know when one sentence ends and another begins so that you can employ the correct punctuation mark. Read the following aloud:

The football authorities are very concerned about agents, they are seen to be profiting from the game and not putting much back into it, naturally sports agents defend themselves against these charges, the impression persists, however, that agents are leeches on the sport

The flow of meaning when you read that passage aloud should have told you that some of the commas inserted are not 'strong enough'. Full stops are required at three places:

The football authorities are very concerned about agents. They are seen to be profiting from the game and not putting much back into it. Naturally sports agents defend themselves against these charges. The impression persists, however, that agents are leeches on the sport.

As there is a full stop after 'charges' and a new sentence begins, 'the' has to become 'The' as the first word of a new sentence. The commas that surround 'however' are correctly used as 'however' is an interjection, a linking word or phrase or a word that is used for emphasis. Common interjections include 'for example', 'however', 'of course', 'nevertheless', 'then', 'on the other hand', 'similarly', 'equally'. When these interjections are used at the beginning of sentences, they usually require a comma after them:

Of course, the evidence is vague.

However, there is another point of view about this issue.

If they are used in the middle of a sentence and they interrupt the flow of meaning, then they require a comma before and after:

The result, nevertheless, was total stalemate.

The opponents of the bill, on the other hand, argue heatedly for total reform.

COMMAS

Commas cause many students difficulties: when to use them, when not to use them. Some students think the best solution is to insert commas all over the place so that their written work suffers from what we might call 'comma-itis', a rash of unwanted commas cluttering up their work. Look at this example:

The rock star, reacted angrily, to the interviewer's questions, and

threatened to walk out there and then, his manager, persuaded him
to stay which the disgruntled singer reluctantly did. The questions,
continued to irritate him however until finally he walked out, later
he issued a statement, denying he had acted out of pique and
blaming, the stupid questions asked by the interviewer.

The correct version is:

The rock star reacted angrily to the interviewer's question and
threatened to walk out there and then. His manager persuaded him
to stay, which the disgruntled singer reluctantly did. The questions
continued to irritate him, however, until finally he walked out. Later
he issued a statement denying he had acted out of pique and
blaming the stupid questions asked by the interviewer.

Note the differences between these two versions. The examples of
'comma-itis', the use of unnecessary and incorrect commas, have
vanished. Look at where commas have been correctly used and decide
why they have been inserted there.

PRACTICE (ANSWERS ON PAGE 157–158)

1. Read the following passage aloud and decide where one sentence
   should end and another begin. Rewrite the passage with the correct
   punctuation.

   Television chefs have achieved a level of fame that is quite
   staggering after all they are only cooks and yet they are treated as
   major celebrities what does this tell us about our present day
   culture certainly we pay too much attention to food and drink we
   forget that half the world is starving while we indulge ourselves all
   these food programmes on television only make matters worse
   celebrity chefs have a lot to answer for

2. The following passage has been attacked by a rash of 'comma-itis'. Rewrite it, getting rid of unnecessary commas and leaving only those that are justified by the meaning.

Reality programmes on television, scrape the barrel as far as entertainment is concerned, the Big Brother programmes, whether they are those series involving so-called celebrities or ordinary members of the public, are particularly crass and, encourage viewers to be voyeurs, watching other people live their lives is, not a healthy pastime for anyone, we are being turned into a nation of couch potatoes, who are more concerned about other people's lives, than our own. Some people, are desperate to be famous, which is why they are willing to do almost anything in front of the cameras, television authorities however should not be encouraging, that pathetic tendency

THE USE OF THE APOSTROPHE

The apostrophe (') is frequently misused and some assessors get very upset about this. One of the most common misuses is *it's* (the abbreviated form of 'it is') and *its* (meaning belong to it). It is amazing how many public notices get these two mixed up. Look at these examples of newspaper headlines:

Its a Record!

It's Wheels Came Off!

In the first example, 'its' means 'it is' so there should be an apostrophe: *It's A Record!*

In the second example, 'its' means belonging to it so there should not be an apostrophe: *Its Wheels Came Off!*

Do not confuse it's and its: it is a bad error.

Apostrophes are usually used to:

1) denote possession and

2) show that a word has been shortened or words combined by the omission of letters.

   My daughter's education has been first class. The school's reputation is second to none. The head's leadership has a lot to do with it.

In 'daughter's', 'school's' and 'head's' the apostrophe denotes possession: of my daughter, of the school, of the head.

Note, however, that when you use possessive pronouns, no apostrophes are required:

   Theirs is over there, yours is here. Ours is black, hers is blue.

Abbreviated form require apostrophes as in don't, weren't, aren't, isn't, won't, can't, shouldn't, wouldn't, couldn't.

PLURALS AND THE APOSTROPHE

Sometimes students insert apostrophes in straightforward plural nouns: this is another bad mistake:

   Wild animal's deserve to be protected from poacher's. Government's and international bodie's must cooperate to put a stop to these cruel practices'.

This should read:

   Wild animals deserve to be protected from poachers. Governments and international bodies must cooperate to put a stop to the cruel practices.

Plural nouns do not require apostrophes unless they are used possessively:

Our friends' houses are much more luxurious than ours.

Politicians' instincts are always directed towards winning popular support.

Women's rights must be protected.

PRACTICE (ANSWERS ON PAGE 158–159)

1. The following passage consists of several sentences without full stops and capital letters where appropriate. Rewrite it inserting full stops and capital letters where required.

   Smoking in public places is an emotive issue opponents of a ban talk of infringements of civil liberties supporters of an outright ban emphasise the health issues involved and the rights of workers employed in the catering and bar trade the majority of the adult population are now non-smokers this fact allows the government to take what formerly could have been a hugely unpopular measure

2. The following passage uses several interjections. Insert commas where you think they are appropriate.

   Firstly there is no proof to back up this thesis. Supporters of the theory however argue that the onus is on its opponents to disprove it. On the contrary the opponents cry, the burden of proof is always on those making the claims. Although the arguments for and against are fairly strident nevertheless it is mainly good-humoured on all sides.

3. The writer of the following passage has been struck with 'comma-itis'. Rewrite the passage deleting all unnecessary and incorrect uses of commas.

Fashion models are often accused, of being stupid and vain. These accusations are usually, without foundation. Models, in fact, have to work hard for their money. It is true, that, many are vastly overpaid for what they do. Nevertheless, they have become, targets for unjustified criticism and sheer, envy.

4. The following passage has numerous incorrect uses of *it's* and *its*. Rewrite the passage using *it's* and *its* appropriately.

Its a problem that can cause stress to it's owner when a pet behaves badly. Its not only an embarrassment, but its not fair on the animal. It's behaviour reflects its state of overall well-being and cannot help but be a reflection on it's owner's handling of the animal.

5. The following passage has numerous examples of missing apostrophes or apostrophes inserted inappropriately. Rewrite the passage with these apostrophe errors corrected.

This is where our neighbours garden ends and our's begins. Their's stretch back to those tree's and ours to those bushe's. Our gardeners lawn mower broke down the other day, so we had to borrow my friends mower. Look at those plants'. They've grown a lot in a year. We cant claim the credit, we just don't have green finger's at all.

17
SPELLING

● ● ● ● ● ● ●

As we have already stated, it is important to minimise the number of spelling errors.

Some common spelling errors are particularly to be avoided:

THEIR/THERE/THEY'RE

Mixing up 'their' with 'there', or vice versa, is a particularly avoidable error.

Remember that 'their' is the possessive adjective:

I went to their house.

It was their special celebration.

This is not to be confused with 'there', which is used to show that something exists or is:

There exists just such a place.

There is no doubt about it.

Or it is used to mean 'in that place':

The office is over there.

There is the exact spot where it happened.

'Their' and 'there' are not to be confused with 'they're' which is the shortened version of 'they are':

They're just appearing in the distance now.

They're arguing because they misunderstand each other.

WERE/WHERE/WE'RE

Similarly, it makes a bad impression if you mix up the three words above.

'Were' is a part of the verb 'to be':

We were out late last night.

The builders were working all day.

'Where' is either used as a conjunction (joining word) or an interrogative pronoun:

I asked where he lived.

Where were you going when this happened?

'We're' is the abbreviated form of 'we are':

We're about to leave.

We're over the moon about this.

Here is a list of words that you should know how to spell correctly because you will use them quite often in your essays:

Absence, absolute, abstract, academic, acceptance, accidentally, accommodation, accordance, accumulation, achievement, acknowledge, acquire, advertisement, affect, alcohol, allege, alliance, alliteration, ally, almost, already, altogether, always, ambiguous, ambivalent, analogy, analysis, ancestors, animal, answer, apparatus, apparently, appearance, appropriate, argument, article, assembly, associated, assonance, assume, assumption, attitude, authority

bankruptcy, barrier, basically, beautiful, because, beginning, behaviour, beliefs, believe, benefit, benefited, between, bias, biological, building, business

campaign, capable, capital, career, catalogue, century, chaos, character, childhood, chronic, chronicle, chronological, collaborate, college, commentary, commission, committee, comparatively, comparison, competent, completely, complement, complimentary, condemn, conflict, conclusion, conscience, conscientious, conscious, consensus, consistent, conspiracy, contemporary, context, contextual, continually, contradictory, corporation, courageous, credibility, criteria (plural), criterion (singular), critical, criticism, cynicism

data, debate, deceit, decision, defence, definite, description, desperate, desperately, detached, deterioration, developed, dialogue, difference, dilemma, disappearance, disastrous, discipline, discussion, disillusioned, dispute, dissolve, division, duel

ecological, ecstasy, effort, eighth, electricity, elusive, embarrassment, endeavour, environment, equivalent, essential, evaluation, evidence, exaggerate, examination, exceed, except, exceptionally, exchange, excitement, exempt, exercise, exhibition, existence, expedition, expense, experience, expertise, explanation, extraordinary, extremely

factors, factually, family, favourite, feasible, feud, financial, followed, foreign, fortunately, fulfil, fulfilment gauge, generalisation, global, globalisation, government, gradually, grammar, grotesque, guarantee, guard, guilty

height, heir, heroes, historical, honesty, honour, honourable, humorous, humour, hypocrisy, hypothetical

identical, identify, identity, illegible, illogical, illusion, illustrate, imagination, immediately, imminent, impossible, incidentally, incontrovertible, independence, indigenous, infinite, ingenious, initial, innate, install, instalment, intellectual, intelligence, intention, interested, international, interpretation, intrigue, invention, irrelevant, island, issue

judgement (also judgment)

knowledge, knowledgeable (also knowledgable)

laboratory, language, lawyer, league, lecture, legislation, leisure, liaison, library, lieutenant, likelihood, literature, logical

maintenance, majority, management, manoeuvre, manufacture, marriage, materially, mechanically, medicine, menial, metaphor, miniature, miscellaneous

naturally, necessary, negate, negation, negative, negligent, negotiate, neutral, neutrality, nullify, numerous

obstacle, obviously, occasionally, occurred, occurrence, omission, opportunity, ordinarily

parallel, perception, periodically, phase, philosophy, physically, population, possessions, practically, practice (noun), practise (verb), prejudice, preparation, pressure, preponderance, prevalent, principal, principle, privilege, probably, procedure, proceed, procession, produce, professional, profit, programme, program (computer context only), progression, prohibit, pronounce, propaganda, prophet, proportion, proposition, protection, psychology, pursue

quality, quantity, query, queue, quiet, quite, quota

reality, receipt, reception, recipe, recommend, reference, referred, regional, religious, repetition, reputation, resistance, responsibility, rhyme, rhythm

satellite, scarcely, schedule, scheme, scholar, science, secretary, selection, separate, shareholders, similarly, simile, situation, source, statistics, special, subtle, succeed, successful, sufficient, suggestion, surprising, suspicious, system, systematic

technical, technique, temperature, temporary, tendency, thorough, threshold, tolerance, tragedy, triumph, truly, typical, tyranny

unbelievable, uncontrolled, unconventional, undeniable, underdeveloped, underrate, undoubtedly, unnecessary, unparalleled, unusual, usually

vague, valid, validation, valuable, valuation, vanguard, variable, variance, vehement, vision

weather, weird, whether, wilful, withhold

PRACTICE (ANSWERS ON PAGE 159–160)

Read the following passages. They contain numerous errors: pick these out and correct them.

1. The reality of the situashion is that the company is facing bankruptcy. The shairholders are demanding action and the summoning of a speshial general meeting. They believ that only by drastic manievres will disaster be averted. They clame that they have been ishuing warnings about this crisas for some time, but they have been ignored. Wether or not the firm can be rescud is very much open to quession. The dets have mounted and the crediters are banging on the door. There demands have to be met as they where unaware of the state of the business when they supplied they're services and goods.

2. A Euro is ruffly equivilent to 70p. However, it is not it's innate value that many British people have reservashions about. It is the surrender of the British currency. Undenibly, this is partly due to an insolar attitude to Europe. The 'Little Englander' stance is still very prevalent in this iland country. Wether this will change in the future is open to dout. Many facters can alter the political whether and what seemed wholly unimaginable a year or so ago can become hard fact overnight. It may be that the British people will give up their resistence to the Euro and the pound will belong to the histirocal past.

18
BIBLIOGRAPHIES AND
REFERENCE LISTS

● ● ● ● ● ● ● ● ● ● ● ● ●

For coursework assignments, it is sometimes
obligatory to list the reference books you have read or
consulted in preparing to write your essay. This is
demanded partly to check that you have not been
plagiarising from these books, that is, copying chunks
of text from them and inserting them in your essay. Plagiarism of this
kind needs to be avoided like the plague: the plagiarised sections will
stand out like the proverbial sore thumb in the surrounding context of
your essay and could lead to your being awarded no grade at all. So, if a
bibliography is demanded, here is how to approach it.

The name of the author of the text comes first in reverse order: surname,
then a comma, then first name and the initial of any other names
followed by another comma:

Peabody, Arthur J.,

Then the title of the book or text printed in italics or underlined:

Shakespeare and His Many Identities

Then comes the place of publication, the name of the publisher and the
date of publication within brackets:

(London: Bergman and Co., 2005).

So the entry would look like this:

> Peabody, Arthur J., *Shakespeare and His Many Identities* (London: Bergman and Co., 2005)

All these details are printed in the book you have used and should be noted at the time of your using it and listed in the reference or bibliography section at the end of your essay.

If you have consulted an essay or unique section of a longer book, then there is a slightly different method of listing this reference.

The author's name comes first (first name, any initial and surname) then the name of the essay or chapter within single inverted commas followed by a comma. Thus:

> 'Significant Developments in Shakespearian Studies',

Then the title of the book in which the section appears: it is best to use italics for this to distinguish it from the title of the section or essay:

> in *A Shakespearian Guide*,

Then 'ed.' to denote 'editor', followed by the name of the editor in the order of first name and then surname:

> ed. Margaret Medway

Then within brackets the place of publication, the name of the publisher and the date of publication:

> (Edinburgh: Scotia Press, 2005)

The last, but important detail is on which pages of the book the essay or section appears:

> pp. 102–112

Thus, the complete entry looks like this:

> Sarah Jones, 'Significant developments in Shakespearian Studies', in *A Shakespearian Guide*, ed. Margaret Medway (Edinburgh: Scotia Press, 2006), pp. 102–112

The amount of detail demanded of reference section and bibliographies will vary according to the level you are working at and the particular demands of the school, college or university at which you are studying.

Make sure you know what the rules are about providing bibliographies and references. Find out what the standard style of listing is for your particular needs and institution and follow those to the letter.

19
EXAMINATIONS

● ● ● ● ● ● ● ● ● ● ●

There is a technique to taking timed examinations in an examination room. Indeed, one of the things you are being examined in when you sit an examination is how good you are at sitting examinations!

Two students can enter the same examination room with the same level of preparation, knowledge and 'feel' for a subject and end up with very different grades at the end of the process. The difference between the two is how each of them meets the particular demands of the exam.

The first golden rule is to give the examiners what they want. Don't have a mental argument with them. Don't bother with thoughts like 'This question is unfair!' or 'Why are they asking me to do this?' Just carry out the instructions of the exam paper to the letter. You can moan and groan about it later!

Before you sit any examination, you ought to be totally aware of the kind of question likely to come up and the areas of knowledge you are to be examined in. Study old examination papers, listen to what your teachers tell you. If anything in the examination paper comes as a surprise to you, then it is probably your own fault.

Read the exact instructions of the exam paper to make sure you know exactly what you have to do. Take these instructions as an example:

Time allowed: 2 hours

You must answer two questions from Section A and one question from Section B.

That is crystal clear: three questions in all, but two from Section A. Any deviance from this will be penalised, so don't take it into your head to answer two questions from Section B because you feel more confident about your ability in that section. That will just not wash!

Pay attention to the mark weighting given to different sections or questions. This will give you a clue as to how you should divide your time in answering the different questions:

What prompts Elizabeth to dislike Darcy on first acquaintance? [8]

Show in detail how Elizabeth begins to change her judgement of Darcy.   *[15]*

The different mark weighting awarded by the examiners to these different sections tells you that you should spend almost twice as long answering the second question as the first.

Dividing up your time in an exam is a crucial part of exam technique. If you are asked to answer four questions and they are given equal mark weighting, then you should spend roughly an equal amount of time on each answer. Even if you think you know far more about two of the questions than the other two, it is a serious mistake to cut down on the time you give to answering the other two.

Consider this: an exam candidate in a two hour examination spends an hour and twenty minutes answering the first two questions, twenty five minutes answering the third and fifteen minutes attempting an answer to the third. Let us assume s/he does well with the first two answers and is awarded 18 out of 25 for both.

155

The third answer is briefer and is awarded 12. The fourth answer is skimpy and rushed and that is awarded 7. That makes a total of 55.

If, however, a roughly equal amount of time had been given to each question, it is possible the first two answers might have been awarded slightly less, say 17 each, but the third and fourth would have made up for that. They are awarded 15 each, making a total of 64, a significant difference.

You have to discipline yourself as far as division of time in an exam is concerned. Don't kid yourself that by answering a question at the end of an exam in note form, adding what you would have covered had you had enough time, will earn you the same marks as if you had written a proper essay answer. Most chief examiners issue instructions that answers in this kind of abbreviated form are marked out of half marks as a total. A question with a mark weighting of 25 would then be marked out of 12 and then the examiner has to assess how well you managed the note form answer and mark out of this total. You are likely to end up with a 7 or 8 at best.

Remember: give the examiners what they want. Read the questions carefully, underlining key words and terms. Obey all instructions about numbers of questions to be attempted from which sections, be disciplined in your use of the time allowed and follow a structured essay plan in your answers.

ANSWERS TO PRACTICE SECTIONS

● ● ● ● ● ● ● ● ● ● ● ● ●

SENTENCES pp. 137–138

a) Women, on average, earn 30% less than men. As government legislation under the Equal Pay Act has obviously not had the desired effect, it is a change in fundamental attitudes that is required. Government may have to use compulsion to equalise pay between the sexes, as economic disadvantage does not help the cause of women's rights, which are supposed to be at the heart of government policy.

b) The majority of filmmakers are hoping to make the ultimate blockbuster. This means that most films have a sameness about them, because they are full of special effects, very loud soundtracks and juvenile content. As a large potential audience exists for more intelligent cinema, film-makers should not underestimate the taste of their audiences, who will, at some point, tire of no-brainer movies.

PUNCTUATION pp. 140–141

1. Television chefs have achieved a level of fame that is quite staggering. After all, they are only cooks and yet they are treated as

major celebrities. What does this tell us about our present-day culture? Certainly, we pay too much attention to food and drink. We forget that half the world is starving while we indulge ourselves. All these food programmes on television only make matters worse. Celebrity chefs have a lot to answer for.

2. Reality programmes on television scrape the barrel as far as entertainment is concerned. The Big Brother programmes, whether they are those series involving so-called celebrities or ordinary members of the public, are particularly crass and encourage viewers to be voyeurs. Watching other people live their lives is not a healthy pastime for anyone. We are being turned into a nation of couch potatoes who are more concerned about other people's lives than our own. Some people are desperate to be famous, which is why they are willing to do almost anything in front of the cameras. The television authorities, however, should not be encouraging that pathetic tendency.

THE USE OF THE APOSTROPHE pp. 143–144

1. Smoking in public places is an emotive issue. Opponents of a ban talk of infringements of civil liberties. Supporters of an outright ban emphasise the health issues involved and the rights of workers employed in the catering and bar trade. The majority of the adult population are now non-smokers. This fact allows the government to take what formerly would have been a hugely unpopular measure.

2. Firstly, there is no proof to back up this thesis. Supporters of the theory, however, argue that the onus is on its opponents to disprove it. On the contrary, the opponents cry, the burden of proof is always on those making the claims. Although the arguments for and against are fairly strident, nevertheless it is mainly good-humoured on all sides.

3. Fashion models are often accused of being stupid and vain. These accusations are usually without foundation. Models, in fact, have to work hard for their money. It is true that many are vastly overpaid for what they do. Nevertheless, they have become targets for unjustified criticism and sheer envy.

4. It's a problem that can cause stress to its owner when a pet behaves badly. It's not only an embarrassment, but it's not fair on the animal. Its behaviour reflects its state of overall well-being and cannot help but be a reflection on its owner's handling of the animal.

5. This is where our neighbours' garden ends and ours begins. Theirs stretches back to those trees and ours to those bushes. Our gardener's lawn mower broke down the other day, so we had to borrow my friend's mower. Look at those plants. They've grown a lot in a year. We can't claim the credit, we just don't have green fingers at all.

SPELLING pp. 149–150

1. The reality of the situation is that the company is facing bankruptcy. The shareholders are demanding action and the summoning of a special general meeting. They believe that only by drastic manoeuvres will disaster be averted. They claim that they have been issuing warnings about this crisis for some time, but they have been ignored. Whether or not the firm can be rescued is very much open to question. The debts have mounted and the creditors are banging on the door. Their demands have to be met as they were unaware of the state of the business when they supplied their services and goods.

2. A Euro is roughly equivalent to 70p. However, it is not its innate value that many British people have reservations about. It is the surrender of the British currency. Undeniably, this is partly due to an

insular attitude to Europe. The 'Little Englander' stance is still very prevalent in this island country. Whether this will change in the future is open to doubt. Many factors can alter the political weather and what seemed wholly unimaginable a year or so ago can become hard fact overnight. It may be that the British people will give up their resistance to the Euro and the pound will belong to the historical past.

INDEX

• • • •